RESOLVE

RESOLVE

Do We Have Time?

WALTER HES

Library of Congress Control Number:		2016921452
ISBN:	Hardcover	978-1-5245-2095-3
	Softcover	978-1-5245-2094-6
	eBook	978-1-5245-2093-9

Print information available on the last page.

Rev. date: 01/12/2016

To order additional copies of this book, contact:
Xlibris
1-800-455-039
www.Xlibris.com.au
Orders@Xlibris.com.au
750126

RESOLVE

The world situation starts to worry more people, including me. Climate change, many wars, huge multi-national corporations, and political inability in most countries to make effective decisions.

This book tries to come up with answers. It shows how the main characters find the solution and the way to convince the world to listen. I hope you will read it with an open mind and give it some honest thought.

Happy reading.

ACKNOWLEDGEMENTS

This book would have never seen light of day if it were not for the people that encouraged and/or assisted me. My thanks go to my family for their patience and encouragement, to my wife Elly and daughter Natacha, for the many hours they spent editing and my other daughter Dominique who read the very first copy and gave me the courage to continue. To Jenny Macaulay and Keith Paulusse for their advice, and to my philosophy teacher, Rene Souery. His comment that my English language needed a lot of work but that Plato would have been proud of the way I used philosophy throughout the book, was very much appreciated. My special thanks go to Herschel Elliott, the author of *A General Statement of the Tragedy of the Commons*, for his very kind letter in which he gave me permission to quote his essay in my novel. It has been essential to the story and was my inspiration for the book.

Many thanks to all,
Walter Hes

CHAPTER 1

Straight after his arrival by plane, Eric jumped in a taxi to be in time for his appointment, which was successfully concluded early morning. The same taxi dropped him off at the hotel in the city centre.

The scenes that confronted him looking out from the taxi during the drive from the industrial area to the centre rendered him speechless. Of course, he was aware that things were not going well in the country but he had not expected that it had gone downhill this quickly in the big city. In the short period since the Great Financial Crisis, there had been a recovery, but it had been short-lived. He never saw anything like the scenes that confronted him now, not in this country! In the worst suburb, they drove through, all he could see was abject poverty. He saw shabbily dressed people begging, and people fighting. Many shop fronts were boarded up and there was hardly any traffic apart from some public transport. Last time he passed through here, there were some beggars and homeless people but nothing like this.

Leaving the hotel after lunch for his next appointment, he could find no taxi and to his regret was forced to walk; luckily, he had some time.

Where had all this come from in such a short time, he asked himself, and where would it lead?

For a while now, Eric had lived more in the office above his factory than at home. A handsome man in his mid-thirties, quite tall and slim with dark hair that already started to grey a bit, and intense blue eyes that took in everything but were now overshadowed by a worried frown.

As well as personal problems, he had deep worries about the rapid declining sales, mainly of his more upmarket products.

He had worked 12, sometimes 16 hours, a day and when he decided to dump most of the luxury products and return to producing the original bars of soap his father had started with, he got into trouble with Union officials for laying off staff, but it had to be done. The main reason for coming to the big city was to secure the materials and equipment he needed for those basic, old fashioned soap bars. That was all done this morning.

The meeting he was now heading for was at an IT company to discuss updating his computer system in the hope of laying off even more staff and maybe lift his own workload a bit as well.

Thinking about the problems the country was facing, he walked briskly towards his appointment. Even here in a more upmarket area he had to dodge some beggars. Unexpectedly, a young man asked his attention:

"Sir, could I please polish your shoes?" The young man's appearance was telling him that this was not a beggar and his speech was cultivated. Not that his shoes needed care but, on impulse, Eric agreed and started a conversation.

"Why are you polishing shoes? You don't appear to be the type that needs to do this kind of work."

"I see it as one of the few ways to earn an honest bit of money", was the answer.

"You appear to be well educated young man. You should be capable of a better job".

"Yes sir, you're right. I tried and am still trying, but there are no jobs. I am only one of hundreds of applicants and who 'you know seems to be more important than what you know.'"

"I realise that what you say is true" Eric said. "We are living in abnormal and worrying times. I was just thinking about it when we met. Our economy is much too fine-tuned; if something goes wrong, the whole system collapses, as seems to be happening now."

The young man agreed.

"I think the reason is our system of government. As it is, they never seem to be able to agree on anything. We have an old-fashioned economic system and nothing happens or changes."

While thinking of what was said, Eric was studying the young man.

He looked like a bit of a nerd with his thin build, pale face with brown eyes behind small glasses, and in need of a good meal. When the job was finished, Eric asked,

"How much do I owe you?"

"A dollar per shoe would be great."

After Eric searched his pockets, he said:

"Sorry, I only have a 20."

The young man did not have enough change but an old woman in rags that was begging nearby heard them and offered to help. The young man showed her the twenty dollars, which she snatched out of his hand. It disappeared somewhere in her substantial bosom while she gave him a handful of small coins.

"Wait a bit, that's not enough!" But she had already turned around, shouting.

"It is all I have" and she took off, much quicker than you would expect of an old woman.

The young man shouted after her and immediately regretted it as it got the attention of a group of unsavoury young guys gathered at a street corner.

One of them got hold of the woman and pulled her along till they were close to Eric and the young man. She shouted while pointing to Eric.

"He got heaps of money!"

"Yeah, you look like it, too" drawled one the big guys, acting as their leader and motioning to let the woman go. "We need it more than you. It's time you rich guys learn to share!"

They started closing in on them, pushing and shoving; he felt a hand in his back pocket and quickly banged his backside against the brick wall smashing the hand against it. The hand disappeared but he was not out of trouble; he delivered a few good punches but it started to look bad when the big guy appeared, ready to hit Eric with a steel bar that could have split his head in two. When he lifted it, the young shoe polisher kicked the man hard in the back of his knee so he collapsed backwards.

In the mayhem that followed, the young man grabbed Eric by the hand and pulled him into a narrow alleyway. However, there was more trouble ahead: apart from some beggars loitering there and people following them, there was a group of people coming from the other side. They didn't look very trustworthy either.

They looked at each other despairingly, when a door burst open and a big man, a cook by the looks of it, banged the lid of a big pot and shouted:

"No more leftovers for you lot!" while he pulled Eric and the young man into safety and quickly locked the door behind them. It was apparently the back door of a small hotel and the big man was indeed its cook who told them how he watched the trouble from the window. They thanked him profusely and introduced themselves to him as well as to each other.

"I won't forget you, Anthony", Eric said to the young man who made to leave through the front door. "You saved my life! I didn't expect you to be so strong!"

Anthony laughed. "I try to keep fit but this was more strategy than strength. It was a pleasure to knock down that brute. I am sure you would have done the same."

While going through his pockets, Eric exclaimed,

"Oh no! My wallet has gone!"

All he had left were a few business cards. He gave one to Anthony and, when Anthony tried to give him the old woman's change, he shook his head,

"No, no, keep it! Please try to come to my factory; there will be a job for you, I promise."

-·-·-·-

CHAPTER 2

Via the kitchen, Eric made his way into the foyer of the hotel where he asked to see the manager.

"I am sorry sir", the clerk told him. "The policy of the hotel is that only guests can see the manager whenever available. You will have to make an appointment."

Not used to people having no time for him, Eric was slightly annoyed.

He gave the clerk his business card.

"Please present my card to your manager."

The clerk returned very quickly.

"Would you please follow me, sir? The manager will see you."

Eric followed him to a neat room containing a large bureau, a comfortable settee on the side, and some filing cabinets along the wall.

A young lady was busy on the computer. Eric was acutely aware that he looked a bit dishevelled, a tear in his jacket and dirty smudges here and there. Although he was not hurt, his body was aching all over from the unusual exercise.

He thought to himself that the manager had a very attractive secretary. Only able to observe her face from the side, he liked the profile with the determined chin and sharp little nose. A blond bob of hair tied in the back into a bun with some loose strands falling over her ears.

Normally, being in the company of an attractive woman would bring him in an agreeable mood but after all that had happened, Eric was impatient and in a curt tone, he asked her if the manager would be long.

"No", she assured him. "Just a minute. I will be with you in a moment".

Eric started to walk up and down impatiently. The young lady observed him with interest while finishing her work. There was an old-fashioned aristocratic quality about him. She stood up holding his business card saying:

"Are you the famous Hans Eric von Sacksenheim"?

"Known yes, but famous?" Eric answered with a slight smile noticing that her oval face with the large green eyes and high cheekbones was just as attractive from this angle. She was athletically built and nearly as tall as him.

"I am sorry I kept you waiting. I had to finish some urgent business. What can we do for you, sir?" she inquired. That took Eric by surprise.

"Are you the manager?"

"Yes, sir" she said smiling, "and the owner as well."

"This is the first time I meet a female hotel manager." Eric admitted, adding apologetically, "Please forgive my manners, and my appearance. I was mugged near your hotel. I am very grateful to your chef and a young man who rescued me, but my wallet and everything from my pockets was stolen. All I'm able to show you is my business card. I hope you can help me?"

"No need to apologise", the manager said. "I am pleased to meet you, Mr. von Sacksenheim. My name is Monica. I am sorry for the welcome New York gave you. We'll see what we can do. First, you may want to cancel your credit card. Please feel free to use my phone. Then we'll figure out what to do."

"Thank you, Monica. Please call me Eric", he answered and went to phone his bank manager while asking Monica if she would like to speak to him to verify his identity. She accepted and received confirmation that her guest was indeed who he said he was.

Monica then picked up the phone and told the clerk in the hotel lobby to book Mr. Eric von Sacksenheim in suite number 2. Then she turned to Eric,

"My uncle and I would be honoured to have your company for dinner. We have it in the dining room at around seven o'clock."

"I would like that very much, thank you", Eric replied. "I will have some time to make a few phone calls and freshen up a bit."

With that, he took leave while he thought by himself, that she was not only the first female hotel manager, but also one of the most practical and good looking ones he had ever met. He collected the key and went to his room. First, he contacted the IT company to apologise for his missed appointment and to cancel it for the time being; then he called the other hotel to have his overnight bag brought here as soon as possible. After he had a quick shower, he made himself a coffee and was finally able to put his feet up for a bit of a rest. His room was tastefully decorated and compared favourably to many hotels he had been before.

He had of course no clean clothes but it had to do. When it was time, he walked unhurriedly to the dining room not wanting to arrive too early. When he asked the head-waiter to direct him to his manager's table, he was told that there was a message that his overnight bag had arrived and was on its way to his room.

Monica and an elderly gentleman were already in deep conversation. Monica's companion was earnestly looking at her over a pair of old-fashioned wire-rimmed glasses balancing on the end of his nose, gesticulating enthusiastically in the air. He was probably in his late fifties or early sixties; his face was crowned with unruly grey hair as well as decorated with a generous beard and moustache, leaving not much uncovered of his friendly face. He reminded Eric of his long-lost grandfather.

Monica, her blond, wavy hair now falling loosely onto her shoulders, had changed from a business outfit to a flattering dress. She looked up and smiled.

"Welcome, Eric. This is my uncle Sebastian. Uncle, please meet Eric von Sacksenheim who I invited to join us. Have a seat, Eric."

Before sitting down, Eric bowed slightly and replied that he was honoured to be sharing a table with such a beautiful lady and her uncle. Monica, while acknowledging the compliment with a gracious nod, complimented Eric on the flower he had attached to the breast pocket of his jacket.

"Thank you, Monica" Eric said, "but I have to confess that this flower was taken from your lobby. I am trying to hide a tear in my suit, a result of the chaos outside. Alas, my original hotel didn't get my overnight bag here in time to allow me to change."

While they were waiting for dinner to arrive, Monica asked,

"Have you decided how to go from here?"

"Well" Eric said, "I am a bit in a hurry to get back to the factory. As you might know, I own a soap manufacturing business. I am going to start a new production line, or better return to how my father started the factory: producing simple, affordable bars of soap. Our research tells us that these will sell better during lean times. I have ordered the materials today. There is a lot of work to be done to get the factory ready before the order arrives."

Sebastian mentioned that he lived not far from Eric's hometown and suggested that they could travel together in his car, as he wanted to leave as well. Eric liked the idea of not having to go through the city again, especially when Sebastian suggested to leave shortly after midnight.

They decided on two o'clock so they could have a reasonable rest. Eric could then use the car to get home after dropping Sebastian off and have it returned afterwards.

Looking with appreciation at the tastefully set table, Eric said, "The setting is beautiful, Monica. Very inviting, but although I would love to indulge a bit, I hope you'll understand that I will just use one of the three glasses I see. We will be driving most of the night."

"You're right" Sebastian agreed. I will stick to one too.

When the prawn cocktails arrived, an amazed Eric asked his hostess.

"Where, for heaven's sake, did you get fresh prawns at a time like this?"

Smiling Monica explained,

"I have a very good chef who not only rescues people in trouble but cooks well and has excellent contacts in the markets and fishing industry. But yes, you're right, it is increasingly difficult to get fresh supply of anything."

Eric told them then what exactly happened that afternoon and how glad he was not to have to face that again. They discussed the awful situation, especially in the centres of the big cities. The men expressed their worry about Monica being on her own, but she brushed that off saying that she was quite capable of looking after herself.

After that, they fell silent, each immersed in their own thoughts until Eric said,

"When I arrived, I disturbed an animated conversation. If it's not about private matters, please continue."

Uncle Sebastian explained that they often discussed problems between ethics and the law.

"For example, when every person in the courtroom knows the accused person is guilty but that person gets off on a technicality. We were also discussing whether the way the Courts work is ethical as it often favours people that are able to pay the ridiculously high legal costs."

Eric raised his eyebrows questioningly. Sebastian continued,

"You see, Monica has a law degree and I am lecturing in political philosophy. It gives rise to many interesting conversations."

Monica, while motioning the waiter to serve the main course, seemed reluctant to continue in that direction and suggested to keep the conversation light. They tried talking about shows and concerts they had attended. That led them to the problems the country was in and they discussed the fact that arts and education were very much affected by the lack of funding.

They enjoyed exchanging views and ideas, the excellent prepared meal and each other's company. Too soon it was time to retire.

"Please give my compliments to the chef", Eric said, getting up.

"This was a delicious meal, enjoyed in such charming company." He refused the offer of coffee.

"No thanks, better not; I am going to try to get a few hours' sleep."

"I will arrange that you get a wake-up call at 1.30. If there is anything else, please call and let me know", Monica said.

"I think I will be fine, but thanks. Good night to both of you.

And Monica, thank you for all your help. I will settle the bill as soon as I'm at my office. I hope we will meet again."

On time, there was a knock on the door and a waiter brought in a tray with breakfast and a pot of steaming coffee. Eric quickly showered and dressed. He only nibbled from the food, but the coffee was great for waking up. Monica's uncle was already waiting for him and led him straight to the garage of the hotel.

Eric was slightly disappointed not to see Monica to say goodbye to, but inwardly scolded himself. Of course, she needed to be rested for a busy day at the hotel, what was he thinking!

-.-.-.-

CHAPTER 3

Sebastian owned a very old Volvo, which Eric offered to drive. With the garage door half opened, Eric, wary after yesterday, cautiously looked up and down the street but all was quiet and they quickly moved out. Eric nearly regretted that he had offered to drive as the old car was a manual. It was a very long time ago since he drove one, but he soon got the hang of it again.

They were going through the outer suburbs when, just before they turned off into the access road to the highway, something unexpected happened. There was a group of people gathered on the footpath next to the road. Suddenly, a woman stepped out with what looked like a baby in her arms and threw the baby in front of the car. Sebastian screamed, "Stop!" but Eric managed to swing the steering wheel and just missed the bundle. However, a man who stepped on the road in front of the car was knocked to the ground. Again, the professor shouted to stop, but Eric gave gas instead and left the scene as quickly as possible. It took them a while before they calmed down a bit.

"It most possibly was a doll and a set-up to force us to stop, so they could rob us blind, if not worse" Eric finally said. "Because I had to slow right down when trying to miss whatever it was, I do not think that man was hit hard, although he will remember it for some time."

"You handled it right, Eric. I am very happy you were behind the wheel and not me."

To change their mindset, Eric asked Sebastian about Monica. It was a subject Sebastian loved to talk about. He told Eric that they had a special relationship since she was a little girl that jumped into his arms on the occasions he visited her parents' home. He was different to people she used to meet as friends of her parents, or in the homes of her school friends. She always plied him with questions about his travels and adventures. Sebastian recalled fondly the blond schoolgirl that came running home when she heard he was there, and told Eric that, although his brother didn't approve of his lifestyle, they were very fond of each other and respected each other's choices.

He finished telling proudly that Monica graduated at Harvard with a *magna cum laude* law degree. However, after learning about the fierce and sometimes nasty competition between graduates and the treatment that newly graduated female lawyers received in the still male dominated law firms, she didn't even consider a couple of very good offers from well-known law firms. She went back to university, this time in New York City, so she could stay with her parents, to study in another area of interest: computer science. Before completing a Master degree, her father suddenly died of a heart attack and she felt obliged to take on the management of the hotel.

"Which she does very well; but I am sorry to hear about her father, your brother", sympathized Eric.

"It was hard when it happened, especially for Monica's mother. She could not bear staying in the house afterwards. After relocating to the hotel for a while, she moved to California where her other daughter lives and her three grandchildren. It has been three years now; life goes on even though you would have liked it to be different."

"I am still a bit embarrassed that I thought Monica was the secretary of the manager", Eric confessed.

"Don't be." Sebastian said laughing. "It happens all the time and she actually enjoys it."

Sebastian confidentially told Eric that Monica would like to sell the hotel and return to university to complete her degree, but considering today's circumstances, she didn't give herself much chance to get a decent price.

They drove quietly for a while until Eric asked about Sebastian's work.

The professor told him he was lecturing part-time at the University of Harvard and often gave guest lectures at other universities.

"I am curious" Eric wondered, "about why you chose to study political philosophy."

"It took a while before I decided to go to university. I was a bit of a rebel growing up, a bit anti-establishment. I spent some time in a hippy commune, went backpacking throughout Asia and Europe; joined protest marches and demonstration, some against war, others for humane treatment of refugees or the environment. In those years, I met many people of different races, ideologies, and nationalities. It opened my eyes and sparked an interest in humanity, and it made me want to find out why the world is as it is, why we do not seem to be able to live together in peace. So I finally went to university, to my parents' great relief. I chose to study philosophy and majored in political philosophy after which I became a lecturer in the hope to influence the next generation to create a better world."

"Then maybe, you can explain to me Sebastian, what is happening to our country?"

"I sometimes despair" Sebastian admitted, "but looking at the history of the human race, I always regain confidence. It must be a development we must go through to become open to new solutions."

They talked for a long while about politics, especially about the government of the day. The professor quoted Winston Churchill,

"It has been said that 'Democracy is the worst form of government' and it is, except for all those other forms that have been tried from time to time." He added, "And he was right, democracy is a bad system especially for progress, but it's the best system we have."

"Why is that so?" Eric asked.

"Well, it's bad because in a democracy you often find that there are usually two, sometimes more, major parties fighting each other for the power to govern, which leaves them little time to really govern. When a party comes in after winning the election, they blame all the bad things on the previous government and the now opposition gives them no chance to do better, and therefore nothing much happens and no progress is made, because effective, but unpopular decisions are seldom made.

"The other thing you must realise is that we are all a product of our upbringing and experience, so everybody is different; the pessimist looks at the people he passes on the street as possibly bad or even dangerous, while the optimist can see the same people as potentially good and friendly. The same kind of thing happens in politics, far-left leaning people often look at all profit making as bad, while conservatives look at all lefties as troublemakers and 'bleeding hearts'; different rulers approach their role differently, depending on their past, education and upbringing. However, democracy is good because it could work well if people were prepared to listen to each other and tried to find common ground. It sometimes, but not often, happens."

"Maybe a benevolent dictator would be more effective", Eric said.

"That's definitively not ideal, either" Sebastian replied. "Did you know that a philosopher once wrote that the first thing a successful dictator should do when he comes to power, is to kill the most important and influential of his opponents, until people get the message of who's the boss, and only then can he become a benevolent dictator."

"That doesn't sound like a solution, I must agree", remarked Eric with a smile. "I better disregard that possibility."

"You can never please everybody", the professor said. "If you look at the wishes of the whole population . . . I'll give a somewhat simplistic sample, some want bigger and bigger salaries to be able to buy larger houses, more cars and other luxuries, while others would be happy just with reliable electricity, running water and a toilet. It's impossible to make everybody happy and hardly possible to get the support of a majority to stay in government for long. You should read up on Plato when he describes the discussions Socrates had with other philosophers about the changes governments go through. A lot of that is still relevant and that was more than 300 years B.C.! Every kind of government seems doomed; even democracies that try to give everybody a voice will create circumstances that give birth to forces that will overthrow it. The notion of an optimal state or world is out of touch with everyday realities. There are just too many fluctuations and variables. Although I personally find greatness in the diversity of people, their races, beliefs, ideals, and values, it does not make it easy to govern well."

Sebastian went back to Socrates who, close to 2500 years ago, already spelled out how a good government was supposed to be formed and how it should work, and he wondered aloud that it is amazing that we still cannot get it right.

The time went quickly. Just before sunrise, Sebastian took over the wheel as it was not too far from his place and he knew the roads well. "Nearly home" Sebastian said and then, "I wonder where that is?" when they both noticed smoke rising in the air. Turning into his street he exclaimed,

"Oh, my God, it's my house!" and stopped the car. Eric and Sebastian jumped out and went to the man in charge of the fire brigade. The first thing they were asked, after identifying themselves, was if there was anybody living there.

Relieved they didn't have to look for bodies, the fire fighter continued to tell them that the house was already fully alight when they were called. They wouldn't be able to save much. The fire was under control but still going, and nobody was allowed near it. It was too early to establish the cause of the fire but it did look suspicious and would be investigated. As often happened lately, he told them, the probable cause was that one or more people had ransacked the house after observing that nobody had been home for a while. They were probably looking for money and valuables and then set the house alight to cover their tracks.

The professor was devastated and hardly able to answer questions about valuables in the house. "Many, many valuable books that cannot be replaced and my stamp collection as well," he said with tears in his eyes. There were some neighbours around who tried to comfort him. They told him that one of them, up early to go to work, had reported it to the police. The fire must have started during the night. They also reported seeing an old car parked at the house last night, but apart from some unusual noises heard, nothing suspicious. The police had left when the fire was under control.

Sebastian returned to the car, quietly shedding tears for his beloved books and at a loss for what to do now. The fire officer asked Eric if he could get the owner to go to the local police station to make a statement.

"It will be important for the insurance", he added.

When Eric got back behind the wheel he offered,

"Why don't you come with me? There is sufficient room in my house and you can stay for as long as you like while considering your options."

After Sebastian calmed down a bit, they drove up to the police station where Sebastian made a statement and gave his contact details, and so did Eric as Sebastian had accepted his kind offer.

The rest of the way was mostly spent in silence, except for Sebastian's sad sighs every time he recalled books or manuscripts that were irreplaceable and now lost forever.

Eric tried to comfort him and mentioned that there was quite a library at the house and that he was welcome to use it.

At a pit stop where they hoped to get a decent lunch, only an 'all day breakfast' menu was offered. The quality was not great but it kept them going for the rest of the way.

Sebastian was quite impressed with the size of the mansion and the surrounding grounds. Eric introduced him to James, his butler, and told James to show Sebastian around, to look after his needs and let him choose his own room. Eric then had to excuse himself, because he had urgent business at his factory. They would catch up tonight at dinner.

While serving dinner, Pam, the cook, a woman of around sixty with a motherly round face and many laugh wrinkles, apologised for the meagre meal, which the professor waved away commenting that he lived on his own. Having his meal prepared for him was a real treat and he was sure to enjoy it.

Turning to Eric, Sebastian told him that he had chosen a room above the garage and already taken an afternoon nap.

"But those rooms are only small. Are you sure you will be comfortable there?" Eric queried.

"Yes, sure, the size is not important. I like it that the bedroom adjoins a small sitting room with a desk, some comfortable chairs, and a great view over the country. It will be a wonderful place for thinking, reading and doing some studies, without disturbing anyone in the main house."

"As you wish. That's settled then. Please discuss lunch and breakfast arrangements with Pam." Eric said, "I will always try to be home in time for dinner, which is usually served around seven."

-.-.-.-

CHAPTER 4

At work the next day, after organising and attending several meetings, Eric got a bit of time to reflect on the last days. A picture of this interesting woman, Monica, kept appearing in his mind. After what he had learned about her, he liked her even more.

He picked up the phone and called Abel Cohen in New York, an old friend. He told him what happened in New York and mentioned that he stayed at a small, charming hotel, which was for sale. He thought Abel might be interested as it looked like a good investment for the future once the economy improved.

"But don't haggle too much, Abel. She is a smart lady and will not sell if she thinks it's not a fair deal."

Sensing Eric's personal interest, Abel promised to consider it while teasing,

"What's this then my friend, have you fallen for a hotel owner? Is she beautiful?"

The days flew past till one early morning, his secretary, Lucille, a smartly dressed older woman, came in and reported that there was a young man waiting for him.

"What does he want?"

"He says you promised him a job. His name is Anthony Sanders."

"Aha, I know him!" Eric said, obviously pleased. "It's a long story, Lucille, I will tell you later. Yes, of course I will see him. Make it eleven o'clock, I should have some time then before lunch. Please have him fill out a job application in the meantime."

Promptly at eleven, after finishing the most urgent tasks, he called his secretary to show Anthony in.

"Welcome, my friend. How are you? I am impressed that you managed to get here, and very glad you did. How did you get here?"

"A bit of hitch-hiking, Mr. von Sacksenheim, but mostly riding my bike and camping. It was OK, the country roads are quite safe."

"I seem to remember that you were living with family?"

"Yes, sir, with my mum. My father disappeared a long time ago. I never knew him and have no wish to now. I didn't want to leave my mum on her own, but she is in a new relationship and they have moved in together. He's quite a nice guy and makes her happy. I think it's a good thing even though I suspect she moved so soon to give me my freedom."

"That was good of her", Eric said. "I hope it works out for them."

He continued,

"You should know, Anthony, that the employment opportunities here are not great. In fact, I need to lay off more people because of restructuring and downsizing; but let me first have a look at your job application."

While he was reading, he asked his secretary to bring in some refreshments.

"Ah, I see that you have a degree in computer programming. That's a great coincidence! The only employee I need urgently is a computer literate person! Because of the fight in the city, I had to cancel my appointment with an IT company to discuss updating our factory computer. Now I'm thinking that you could help me out here.

What do you say?"

Hesitantly, Anthony replied,

"Please understand that I have no on-the-job experience. I did pass with honours and have been practicing a lot on my own computer. I would love to give it a go."

Then Eric explained that he was in the process of changing production back to simple soaps and needed the computer to facilitate that and adjust the administration part.

"I hope our computer will not be too old for the change. It will be a while before the ordered materials will arrive, so there will be time for you to get to know our system and tell me what you think. You're most welcome to board with me for the time being. I will pay you a basic salary while you can do some jobs for me around the house until we need you at the factory. Use your bike to spend part of the days in the factory office to prepare. I will give you some information, so you can start thinking about programming. Come along with me so I can show you around."

Passing his secretary, he stopped to tell her that Anthony saved him from being hurt in the city and to call his home to tell them to prepare for an extra guest. Lucille had already been working for his father and had obviously been wondering what was going on. Her face broke into a welcoming smile saying that she hoped he would like working with them.

While sharing a quick lunch in the factory's cafeteria, Eric introduced Anthony to the factory supervisor as the next computer specialist who would start full-time as soon as the ordered materials arrived. He left Anthony in his care for the rest of the day so he could explain the production process and introduce him to the other personnel.

On their way home, late that afternoon, Anthony's head was full of all he had seen and heard. What impressed him most of all, he said, was that the factory generated its own electricity by drilling deep underground into the hot rock, then pumping water into the hole and making electricity with the resulting steam. It showed Eric that his new employee was a keen observer. He explained a bit more to Anthony.

"We were very lucky that the factory complex was built above hot rocks not too far below the surface. We have more than sufficient energy and if you look there and there", Eric pointed out, "I am busy installing a power line to the house as well because the outside electricity supply is becoming so unreliable."

Arriving at the house, Eric introduced Anthony to professor Sebastian, James, and Pam. James showed him the guest room he could use, and Anthony left to freshen up for dinner.

While they enjoyed a drink, Eric explained to the professor that Anthony was the young guy he told him about before.

At the dinner table, Anthony related his experiences at the factory to the professor and told him enthusiastically about the electricity supply.

"Imagine, sir, your own reliable electricity for nothing!"

"Not exactly" Eric commented, "the generator alone costs more than ten years of outside supply, but so far it is more reliable and in the end, it will pay itself."

The professor told them that he had discovered the greenhouse at the back of the vegetable garden and confessed that he was a bit of a gardener, expressing regret that he would now never be able to show them the beautiful orchids in his own garden, as it was probably totally ruined.

"You could use the greenhouse much more effectively, if you don't mind me saying so", he remarked.

"Yes, I know" Eric agreed. "I had to cut down on some garden help. My head gardener is now on his own, and he only comes in three days a week. He cannot do it all, so it's mainly Pam, our cook, that looks after the greenhouse and the kitchen garden. She does not have enough time either. If you want to turn your hand to it, you are most welcome and Anthony is now free to help. Just let James know whatever it is you need and he will try to get it delivered. But", he added with a wink, "before you start on exotic orchids, let's concentrate on becoming self-sufficient in food supply for now and next winter. Our Pam is very good in preserving fruit and vegetables."

While talking, it had become quite late and Eric noticed that Anthony started to look very tired.

"I think it's high time we break up. Anthony, we usually start breakfast at seven, although I might have gone by then, but please, sleep in if you like; you had a very tiring couple of days. Pam will make you breakfast when you get up."

Eric and Sebastian talked bit longer while finishing off the bottle of wine. Eric asked the professor if James had shown him the library and if it would be useful to him.

"Yes, I checked it out and I am impressed with the great variety of quality books you collected, even some good books on philosophy. I took one book to read before bed, but during the day I will spend some time on work I need to finish for my lecturing job at Harvard. It's convenient that the holidays just started. After the holidays, I will return to Boston where I have accommodation at the campus", adding that he was also keen to start on the greenhouse, especially with some help from Anthony.

"Great!" Eric said. "I don't think you have met the gardener. His name is Gerald. If you can spare Anthony sometimes, he will be happy with an extra hand too."

Both men declined a coffee and retired to their rooms.

About four weeks later when Eric got home from work, he got another surprise: there was a brand-new BMW convertible parked in front of his house, and Monica and Sebastian were talking on the porch. It was obvious that she had just arrived. They saw him and were waiting for him to join them.

"Well, well", Eric said. "Who have we got here!" He greeted Monica warmly.

Monica looked like a teenager on her birthday and was positively beaming. She started to tell her story when Eric interrupted,

"I think this calls for a celebration! It is still nice weather, let's sit on the back terrace while you continue the good news, and share some refreshments."

While James took care of drinks and some snacks, Eric asked Monica if she could stay for dinner and added that she was also most welcome to stay the night.

"Yes, please. I would like that very much", she answered.

Then Anthony showed up and was introduced to Monica. Finally Monica got the chance to continue with her story.

"A few days after you left, a gentleman by the name of Cohen came to the hotel to talk to me."

"Did he make an appointment?" Eric interrupted with a cheeky smile. "I remember that one can only see the manager by appointment!"

Monica laughed.

"As a matter of fact, he did, saying he might be interested in buying the business. To make a long story short, after I took him around the hotel and showed him the books, he seemed impressed and made me an offer which was half a million less than I had hoped. He said that in todays climate, he could only offer me three and a half million. I said I would think it over and was planning to discuss it with you, Uncle, and of course Mom and sis. However, the next day he called and said,

'I'll make it four if you say yes now.'

"Of course, I did then, I could not believe my luck! We got the lawyers involved who drew up a contract, which I signed. The deposit was paid and five days ago, the whole amount was deposited in my bank account, believe it or not! I finished all that had to be done and I am very pleased that, as far as I know, all personnel will keep their jobs."

Monica was a bit breathless after relating the news in one go, and paused before adding triumphantly:

"I am free! And I spoiled myself buying the car I always wanted but could not afford. I didn't call you, Uncle, I wanted to surprise you personally with good news after that awful fire. Are you pleased?"

Sebastian hugged her.

"Could not be more pleased! Congratulations, my dear girl, so happy for you! What are your plans now?"

"I would like to spend some time with you, Uncle, but I don't want to impose now you are living here in Eric's house. I also would like to travel a bit and see something of the world before finishing my degree."

"Imposing! Rubbish!" Eric exclaimed. "I am also very happy for you and you can stay here if you wish. Take your time to decide what to do now. We'd love you to join us; we need female input into our discussions at the dinner table. Please stay and make yourself at home. James will show you our guest rooms."

"If I may suggest" said Sebastian, "It would be great if Monica stayed in the other room above the garage, close to me, so we can share the sitting room and talk a bit more."

"Are these rooms still called 'stable boy rooms'?" Monica asked cheekily.

"Well", Eric smiled. "You're right. They were meant for the stable boys when we still had horses in the stables. That's why they are the smallest bedrooms in the house. And not very lady like."

Monica laughed and said that she would be very happy to stay there for the time being.

All during the conversation, Anthony had been studying Monica and then he blurted out,

"I think I've seen you before, Miss. Could that have been at the computer school of New York University?"

"That's quite possible", Monica answered. "I studied there for a master's degree in computer science which I unfortunately was not able to complete. What did you study?"

Anthony told her that he studied for a bachelor's degree in computer programming and graduated last year.

"I had high hopes it would help me find a job, but didn't succeed until I was so lucky to meet Mr. Eric."

"I was just as lucky meeting you", Eric said, and turning to Monica he added,

"Anthony is the one that floored the brute that was about to hit me with an iron bar. Not only did he save my life, showing character and courage, but he crossed my path just at the time I needed a programmer for my factory computer."

They then broke up to change for dinner. At the dinner table, Eric told his guests how he enjoyed having company for dinner these last few weeks. He then raised his glass to welcome Monica and said that he would now enjoy it even more.

Sebastian responded for all, expressing their gratefulness for the hospitality that was offered at the drop of a hat. He added that he enjoyed working with Anthony to put the greenhouse to good use in collaboration with Gerald, the gardener.

"Such a nice guy", he said, "and really happy to receive a bit of help. I think the greenhouse is now all set up to supply you with produce at least for the rest of the year."

"That's great" Eric replied, "I will soon need Anthony at the factory."

Eric asked Sebastian if he had received more news about the fire.

Sadly, there was only bad news concerning his books and papers. Monica suggested that she and Sebastian would soon drive there to check things out for themselves.

-·-·-·-

CHAPTER 5

Dinnertime was usually the only time of the day the four of them were together as Eric worked most weekends too. They often discussed the dire economic situation the country seemed to be bogged down in. How could it be that their beautiful country had come to this? They always came back to the same conclusion that the government and the two-party system were mostly to blame but, although they played with several ideas, they couldn't agree on a solution. Then, one day, Anthony made a remark that made them all sit up:

"I think a computer could do a better job than those overpaid people that are supposed to lead the country!"

Although they laughed at first, it made everybody think.

"Is that a silly idea or would it be a possibility? What do you say, Monica?" Eric asked.

"Maybe" she responded hesitantly, "the idea is worth thinking about and exploring. You would need a supercomputer of course.

Enormously expensive to buy, as well as to maintain."

Sebastian cautioned,

"A computer would not be able to make a government popular. Remember, Eric, that I told you that it will never be possible to please everyone."

"It shouldn't be about pleasing everyone, Sebastian, we need a good functioning government that finds solutions instead of more disagreement."

A few days later in his office, Eric called the IT company manager he was going to see in New York. "I am sorry I had to cancel, Brian. In the meantime, I'm afraid I have changed my mind. Tell me, would it be possible to acquire a supercomputer?"

"You want what?" Brian said incredulously. "You do not want a supercomputer; you don't need it! Do you realise you would need a special building for it with a fail-proof cooling system? The price alone will be prohibitive and apart from that, it will cost you a fortune in power alone!"

Taken aback but not totally discouraged, Eric kept thinking about it in the weeks that followed.

Pam took to mothering Anthony a bit. They had taken a real liking to each other, which led Anthony to ask Eric if it was OK for him to have his dinner with her in the kitchen. Throughout his university studies, Anthony lived at home with his mother and he was missing her care, her interest in his life and the practical things, like replacing buttons, etc. Pam on the other hand, was a woman that loved looking after people. She had been widowed long time ago and her grown-up children lived all over the country, none close-by. Eric understood that Anthony would be more comfortable in Pam's company and told him that it was a great idea. He was going to ask him anyway to help Pam in the kitchen a bit, especially to keep the fire going until the electricity would be connected. However, on some occasions he might ask him to join them at the dinner table.

A few days later, while enjoying a drink before dinner, waiting for Sebastian to join them, Monica asked,

"Did my uncle tell you that I would like to sell the hotel?"

"As a matter of fact, he did, and because I liked your hotel and thought it an asset for anyone, I told a friend about it. I am glad it worked out. He wouldn't have bought it, if he did not think it was a good deal. I haven't heard from him yet, so it was a real surprise when you turned up."

Monica got up and gave him a spontaneous hug.

"I knew it, I knew it! Thank you so much. You have been so good to both of us, how can we ever repay you?"

"Don't mention it", Eric said. "I am a lonely man and really enjoy all your company. I hope you are enjoying yourself too and are not in a hurry to leave."

"I am having a wonderful time! Uncle and I have long walks and even longer talks. We have been back to see what's left of his house.

The fire was caused by arson and they're still hoping to find the culprit, but there's so much crime now that I don't think there is much hope. Apparently, the bookcases were overturned that's why it burned so fiercely. Few books were spared and none undamaged. Nothing else left either. Thankfully, my uncle was well insured, although many of those books are irreplaceable. But he is not sad about having to move from there. He was hardly ever there and now thinks of moving to Boston permanently."

Sebastian joined them and asked Monica if she heard from Chris.

"Not yet." she answered, turning to Eric.

"Chris was my chef, a good man and an excellent cook. I am disappointed that the new manager decided to bring his own chef.

Chris is looking for another position which is not easy these days."

"Another person I owe my life, too" Eric remarked. "I will see what I can do to help; give me some time."

The holidays were nearly finished and Sebastian left for Boston to go back to his part-time lecturing.

Pam had told Anthony about Eric's unhappy marriage that ended with the disappearance of his wife more than a year ago. She thought that Eric and Monica seem to like each other a lot and how good it would be for Eric to be in a new relationship. They conspired with James to arrange a special romantic dinner now Sebastian was away, decorating the table with flowers and candles.

When the couple entered the dining room, they paused and laughed. "What have they been up to?" Eric wondered. "I think somebody likes to play Cupid!" and he offered his arm to Monica. "May I lead you to your seat, my lady?" Monica smiled and put her hand on his arm.

"Thank you", she said gracefully with a little nod.

They enjoyed a delicious dinner. Eric looked admiringly at Monica, whose beautiful features were enhanced by the candlelight. Noticing his look Monica inquired,

"Is there no Mrs. von Sacksenheim? I apologise for the personal question but, considering the setting . . .", she said gesturing towards the table and decorations, ". . . it seems appropriate. Also, I noticed that you are wearing a wedding ring."

"Please feel free to ask any personal question that is on your mind. I have no secrets. Yes, I was married, that's true, but I don't consider myself married any more, although we did have some happy times at the beginning. We married too young. There was some pressure from both our families, especially as my father had not long to live. After my father's passing, another downturn in the economy happened and I worked night and day to keep the business going. Esther just wanted to go out and spend money, lots of money. She couldn't understand times were changing and we had to be more careful if we wanted to maintain our wealth. We had some fights about that and I admit I am not the easiest person to live with. I am a bit of a workaholic and because I was unhappy at home, I spent even more time at the factory.

"A year ago, maybe a bit longer, I came home to find a note saying that she couldn't stand it anymore and went traveling. Now and then I received a card, usually including the message that she was not ready to come home yet. Last time we talked, I asked her to return soon so we could discuss our future.

"For about six months, I paid her travelling bills and then I got a call from a hotel in Italy. They wanted to know if they should keep her room as she had not returned for a week. I tried calling her cell phone repeatedly, but the thing seemed to be dead. I reported her missing and even sent a private detective to find out what happened, with so far, no result other than that she went on a gondola trip and didn't return. After that, nothing . . ."

Monica put her hand on his arm saying how sorry she was to hear that and apologised for bringing it up.

"Don't worry too much, Monica. Of course, I am concerned. She was part of my life but to be honest, it was a relief when she left. I am still hoping to hear from her, especially for her parents sake. Her brother has travelled there and we got the Consulate involved, all with no result. Fortunately, we had no children."

"Enough of that", Eric continued. "I have happier news to tell. If the chef that worked for you . . . his name is Chris, right? If he's interested, he could work for me. I know it's not like a hotel and it could be temporary, but it will give him and us time to find permanent solutions."

"Oh, you are a marvel!" Monica exclaimed.

"It was not a problem, Monica. There were going to be some changes anyway. I had a word with Pam. You know, she is getting on a bit and is somewhat overwhelmed by having to cook for and look after six people instead of the three she has been used to for the last year. On top of that, she is not looking forward to work with the new electrical appliances that have been installed. If Chris accepts, Pam can finally take a long holiday to visit her three children and grandchildren. They live in different parts of the country. When she returns, she will work less hours and spend them assisting James with household chores. That makes him happy too, especially", he said with a wink, "as there is now a brand-new BMW to wash, polish and look after!"

Monica laughed saying that she'd be happy to do that herself. The meal continued in a happy mood, finishing with a coffee on the terrace, as it was a beautiful evening.

CHAPTER 6

Shortly afterwards, Monica announced that she was going on an overseas trip, stopping first in California to see her mum and sister. Apart from catching up, they had some money matters to settle after the sale of the hotel, which was part of her father's inheritance. After that, she would fly to Europe. One of her best friends had invited her to come to Tuscany in Italy to attend her wedding to an Italian guy.

Monica was excited about the invitation and looking forward to attending the wedding.

After the wedding, she planned to spend some time sightseeing through Italy.

James brought her to the airport as it wouldn't be safe to leave the BMW in the airport parking for long. She arrived a few days before the wedding and had a great time catching up with her friend Kate and family.

They studied law together and got to know each other's families well. It was a beautiful three-day wedding in a romantic castle with many guests. Monica enjoyed herself immensely and picked up a bit of Italian while trying to talk to other guests.

After the wedding, Kate went on her honeymoon and Monica went to Rome to visit all the well-known landmarks taking lots of photos. Italy was still trying to cope with huge international debts under ever changing governments. It was easy to find places to stay as tourism was down and hotels and other businesses were eager to get customers. Talking to locals, Monica heard that the influx of refugees that had flooded the country for decades showed no sign of slowing down. But, it seemed to her, the Italian character was better able to cope with bad times than the average American. They mostly stay cheerful and so the tourist is still able to enjoy the atmosphere, although keeping an eye on handbags and luggage was always advisable.

On a whim, Monica decided to go to Venice to see if Eric's private investigator was still on the case.

She thought she'd better call Eric to get some details. Eric was not at all happy about it and worried about her safety, but she waved that away.

"I'm a lawyer, I know what I am doing, trust me. It seems silly to be here and not to check things out for you."

"Oh well, all right then", Eric said. "I do appreciate it, but please be careful."

He told her the name of the detective and the hotel he'd been paying for.

The water taxi brought her from the airport straight to the hotel where the detective was supposed to stay. It was still early afternoon so she decided that before booking a room, she would have a drink in the bar and check things out. She asked the receptionist to look after her suitcase as she had not decided yet if she would stay. After freshening up a bit in the lady's, she went to the bar where she found a small band playing and a group of noisy tourists. While discussing what to order with the barkeeper, she made sure most heard her American accent. As she'd hoped, it worked: a plump little man at the corner of the bar lifted his glass and said,

"Cheers, compatriot."

Monica lifted her glass in response, which the man interpreted as an invitation. Grabbing the bottle of whiskey that was standing next to his glass, he came over and introduced himself as Ben Homer. Happy with her good luck, Monica engaged him in animated conversation about Italy, Europe, the world in general, and then asked him if he was on holiday too.

"No" he said, "I work from here." He asked her about her life in the USA.

"I own a small hotel in New York City", she told him. "Business is very slow now. My manager is quite capable to look after it so I can take a break now and then. This time to see a bit of Europe."

"What are you drinking?" he asked, while signalling the barkeeper.

"Later maybe", she said. "I just started my gin and tonic."

She asked him what kind of work he was doing in Venice and she heard that he was a private detective.

"Very interesting", Monica said.

"Not really", he responded. "I have to find somebody's wife."

"Well" remarked Monica with a wink. "You're not looking very hard in here with that whiskey bottle so handy, are you?"

He laughed.

"You're right but this wife doesn't want to be found! And I don't mind if the bills are paid! In fact, I cannot prove anything yet, but I am as good as certain that she is quite dead!"

"Wow", Monica exclaimed. "How sad! Can you tell me about it?

Accident or murder? How interesting to meet a real sleuth!" He liked that and sat a bit straighter.

"Yes, I can tell you a bit, but let me buy you a drink first."

Monica accepted this time.

The polishing of his ego, her big innocent eyes and another glass of whiskey or two loosened his tongue:

"She was, or is, a rich, bored and unhappy American tourist looking for attention. She fell hook, line and sinker for a gondolier who was only too happy to help her spend money. They had an affair and she bought lots of things for him, the last thing was a motorboat.

Something must have happened on their first trip as she never returned to her hotel." Monica asked him why he was still here then and if he told his client about it.

"I did send a report, but there is no confirmation of her death and the police are not very helpful."

"What a story", Monica said. "It must have been quite an attractive gondolier; did you get to talk to him?"

"Ha" sneered the detective, "you don't know the Italians, very protective of each other. Nobody wants to give information and every other gondolier is called Mario. They're all sexy buggers, aiming for the tourist dollars. I heard all this through people's gossiping. Her husband told me that he put a lot of money into her account to pay for a boat. I found out that the damaged boat was towed back to the boat company by the police who told them to return the boat to the rightful owner." Urged by Monica, he continued with the story.

"The boat company tried to find Mrs. von Sacksenheim but did not succeed or try very hard. She only paid a deposit so they left it at that; it would just about pay for the repairs, they declared. The police admit there was a fatal motorboat accident out of the safe harbour. The official report stated that the woman that died was a nameless prostitute. Do you believe it? I don't! I will keep trying to find this Mario, if the husband keeps paying."

Ben Homer tried to get her to agree to have dinner with him, but she excused herself, saying she was not feeling too good. She pretended that the jet leg was starting to affect her and she did not feel like eating. Maybe they could meet later or tomorrow.

Instead of booking a room, she got her luggage and asked the receptionist to call a water taxi to bring her to another hotel. She complimented the hotel for the happy atmosphere, but that she would like to stay at a quieter hotel, as she needed to recover from an illness. She would love to come back another time. The receptionist apologised for the loud music and helpfully gave her advice about hotels nearby.

Very soon she was underway, enjoying the short water taxi trip. She then had a relaxing dinner on her own in a comfortable and pleasant hotel. She thought about calling Eric to report the meeting with the detective and advise him to stop paying this useless man, but decided to wait a bit till she found out more. Retiring to her room for an early night, she reflected happily on the events of the first day. She had taken the first hurdle and got some information to continue her search.

Early the next morning, she asked around for a gondolier called Mario and discovered quickly that too many of them went by that name, Ben Homer had been right about that. She decided to try to find more information while enjoying being a real tourist and for a few days she booked with different gondoliers to admire the sights. While sharing the gondolas with other tourists, she couldn't ask too many questions but still learned a lot about the life of a gondolier. Most of them, not used to people that were interested in them personally, were happy to explain how and why they started to work as a gondolier, about their families and where they lived.

Monica particularly got along well with one of the older ones and decided to book his gondola for herself, explaining that she would like him to show her Venice, as he liked it best. He loved that and took her to interesting places that were not overrun by tourists while telling her about their historic significance. He told her that Venice in the old times used to be the richest city and the banker of all trade in the then known world, but was now disappearing slowly under water.

She asked about the community of gondoliers, if they were all friends and socialized together. In response, he told her that he and his family had made many good friends who referred customers to each other or offered help in case of health problems, but there were also gondoliers that only looked out for themselves and tried to take business away from others.

On the last day she spent with him, she told him that she was trying to find a good- looking gondolier by the name of Mario, but that she already found out that many gondoliers were answering to that name.

"Don't tell me", the older man said mockingly. "Has sexy Mario broken another American heart?"

"Not yet", Monica laughed. "But I would very much like to see him."

"If you haven't fallen in love with him, may I ask why you are looking for him?" Monica was not prepared for this question and had to make up something on the spot.

"I am a recruiter for an American movie studio. One of the directors did a gondola trip with this man during a family holiday last year. He was impressed with his personality and found him very handsome. I think his teenage daughter fell in love with him, so he took her hastily back to the States. He only remembered his name but is convinced that he is just the right type for a role that has come up.

Do you think he'd be interested?"

"I think I know the one you are looking for and yes, he will be very keen. I will tell him you are looking for him, but do not trust him, he will only try to get as much out of it as he can. Please do not tell him that I warned you. You have been good to me and I don't want you to be taken advantage of."

The very next day, when she walked through the lobby, the clerk called her and told her that there was a gondolier waiting for her outside, insisting that she was looking for him.

"*Gracie*", she said and went outside to finally meet the one she had come to see. She had gone over and over in her mind how she was going to play this and hoped it would be the right tactic. It would be interesting, but she had to be very careful. She greeted him:

"*Ciao*, did Paulo send you? Are you the Mario I'm looking for?"

"*Si, si*, I am. You lady from Hollywood?" Mario asked.

Monica had to admit that this was one hell of a handsome guy: pitch-black hair, liquid eyes overshadowed by long eyelashes, a winning smile and athletic body. His self-assured posture showed that he knew it too!

"No, I am not from Hollywood, but from a recruiting company in New York", she said. "However, we do work for Hollywood's Movie Studios. I suppose Paulo told you why I was looking for you. Would you be interested?"

"Think so, *signora*."

"In that case, we can talk it over during lunch. Can you bring us to a quiet restaurant?"

"*Capito!*" was Mario's enthusiastic response and with a gracious gesture, he offered his hand to help her into his gondola and swung the boat around. He chose a beautiful restaurant and they were shown a table in a quiet corner with a great view over the Grand Canal. It was a bit too early for lunch but certainly not for an *aperitivo*, so they ordered a glass of Campari while the kitchen sprung into gear. Unused to this kind of situation, Mario was a bit uncomfortable, but the drink helped to loosen him up, especially when there was plenty of time for a second one, which Monica declined

"You, *signora*, say I can play in American movie?"

"It could be possible. Of course, your English needs to improve. Don't worry, you will get help with that, but don't you lose that sexy accent! Before we go any further, you will have to tell me a bit about your life."

Mario was happy to tell her during lunch that he was born in a small town not far from Venice and that his father had been a gondolier. He followed in his footsteps from a very young age and did not have much schooling. On the streets, or better canals of Venice, he learned most of what he needed to know about life. No, he was not married, he had too much fun and, with a wink, he liked the signorina tourists too much. He always showed them a very good time. He would love to show Monica a good time too, if she wanted that."

Monica said laughingly,

"I heard a bit of your reputation and might take you up on that, but today I have no more time."

She did not want to overdo it on the first day and promised to have more time the next day. He could take her to all his favourite spots, while they talked some more.

The next day, she found out that Mario was not only very charming company but that he knew the city inside out. Yes, a lonely woman on holiday could quite easily fall in love with him. He showed her the most fascinating palaces, little arches and mosaic art and the great water works a Dutch company was building to protect the city from going under. It was a very warm day, so Monica had decided that shorts with a sleeveless low-cut top were not out of place. She also thought it might encourage Mario to try to come on to her. It seemed to work as several times she caught his eyes wandering.

Late afternoon, Mario suggested to take her to a small, intimate restaurant for dinner where they served the best seafood platter in the whole city.

"I would like that", Monica said. "Take me to my hotel first so I can change. I cannot go to dinner in shorts!" Mario pretended to be surprised.

"This is Italy, *signora*, with legs like *signora's*, all Italian men welcome you to his *ristorante*!"

"*Scusami*" Monica said, "*ma volere* look *molto* better when you take me to dinner."

"*Fantastico*!" Mario exclaimed. "*Signora parla un poco Italiano*.
We have beautiful night!"

Monica took her leave with a smile and let the word 'night' instead of "dinner" ride. She was thinking the relationship might escalate more quickly than she had expected but then again, she was in Italy and Italian people are passionate so she decided to be prepared, putting on her most sexy underwear. After some deliberation about the ethics of her plan, she shrugged her shoulders and took two of the sleeping powders her doctor had prescribed to help her sleep on the plane. It would not do any more harm than to put a dent in his arrogance.

An hour later, Mario was waiting for her in his gondola. He whistled when he saw her as she had dressed sexily but tastefully in a black, body-hugging top with a very wide and long multi-coloured skirt that had a long split, sometimes showing up a bare leg. He had also changed into a classic white Italian shirt and black trousers. Without his jail striped shirt, he did not look like a gondolier anymore. He said admiringly,

"You are very beautiful *signora*" to which she replied:

"You don't look bad yourself, *signore!*"

She half wished they could have a carefree night. She didn't like what she planned to do and had to remind herself that she needed him to talk and that he didn't deserve consideration.

Being out of uniform did not make any difference to his ease in commanding the small boat. He even surprised her by singing an amorous Italian love song to her with a beautiful tenor voice.

As promised, the small hotel/restaurant was indeed intimate and romantic. Low lighting, with candles adorning the table and a guitarist singing sentimental songs. After an *aperativo,* they ordered dinner, or rather Mario did as he suggested:

"*Per favore*, I order, *si?*"

Monica left the table to go to the lady's and stopped in the lobby to reserve a suite for the night, including a bottle of champagne and two glasses. The clerk was very helpful and not at all surprised.

Dinner passed in happy chatter while they enjoyed the amazing seafood platter. Monica could not think of a shellfish that was not represented. There was other seafood as well, accompanied by several delicious fresh salads. Too much food though, accompanied by several wines. Monica made sure Mario drank at least twice as much as she. This was followed by dessert and coffee, both presented with liqueurs.

During dinner, Mario tried several times to get more information about the movie he would play in. Monica said he had to be patient; she was in touch with her people in the U.S. A cameraman would be coming over soon to take some shots of him and a short video. She would give him some lines to remember and they would practice a short scene, but she had not received any details yet. For now, they should use the time to get to know each other better.

She didn't have to tell Mario twice. There had already been some tentative touches of legs, feet, and hands. Monica didn't discourage it so Mario got bolder and when he excused himself to go to the bathroom, he stopped behind her and gave her a kiss on her hair, whispering,

"You are so beautiful, *molto* sexy! I would like to sleep with you!"

Monica said she had reserved a suite for them but hoped they would sit here a bit more with their coffees and liqueurs. Monica tried raising the subject of Esther, but didn't get anywhere at first. She said that somebody told her that he had a terrible experience with a client having a fatal accident.

"You poor thing" she said, "do you want to tell me what happened?"

All she could get out of him was that Esther was a stupid woman.

"Was she American too?" Monica asked.

"*Si*, she was and beautiful too but she was *stupido,* not like you! Not talk about bad time, Mario want to talk *amore*!" Swaying slightly, he got up and offered her his arm:

"Come my beautiful lady, come with Mario."

They picked up the key and went up to the suite, each with great but different expectations. Mario couldn't keep his hands off her and kissed her passionately in the elevator. She leaned into him and said softly,

"Take it easy, *signore*, we have the whole night."

The champagne was waiting for them, chocolates on the pillows and flowers throughout the suite. They toasted to the night, turned the radio to soft dance music and danced a slow dance. Mario rubbed against her letting her feel how turned on he was. She whispered,

"I want to surprise you, please go to the bathroom for a few minutes."

With an understanding laugh full of expectation, he disappeared. Quickly, Monica poured another two glasses, hers half champagne half water. To Mario's glass, she added the contents of the small sachet, unnoticeable in the bubbly liquid. Then she took off her top and skirt, revealing a lacy bra that only partly covered her breasts and a G-string, made of glittering material. Then she draped herself on the sofa waiting for Mario to emerge, her shawl strategically covering her from navel to the top of her legs.

When the bathroom door opened, she was in for an Italian treat: Mario emerged with a rose, taken from the display in the bathroom, between his very white teeth, dressed only in a tiny speedo that, it must be said, had quite a supporting job to do. Monica smiled and said:

"My romantic Romeo, come here, you sexy man and put that rose away as you won't be able to sing, to kiss me, or to enjoy this drink with me."

Seeing Monica's encouraging outfit and her suggestive pose, his eyes had grown big and with a grand gesture, that did not quite come off, he offered her the rose, and unsteady on his legs, he nearly fell next to her on the sofa.

"Ah Monica, Monica, *per favore* be my Juliette, forget drinking, this Romeo wants you!"

But she insisted on a drink first, holding up the glass that was ready for him for another *saluti*. In a hurry, he drank it in one go. Then he turned her face to him and kissed her deeply while his hands roamed over her body, till one hand started to fondle her right breast while the other wandered to the back and unfastened her bra, setting her firm breasts free.

"Come Juliette, come to bed with Romeo and we make beautiful Italian *amore*."

Monica allowed herself to be led by Mario, or was it the other way around? On the bed, more cuddling and kissing. Mario's hands became more insisting, trying to remove her G-string as well, but Monica said her breasts needed attention. She guided his head onto her shoulder and pleaded.

"*Per favore*, make love to my breasts first. I like that so much; it makes me really hot."

Normally, Mario would have forced himself on a woman by now, but the drinks had made him very slow and mellow while the sleeping powder slowly started its intended work. He became very relaxed, sucking her breast.

Monica asked him to tell her sexy stories while stroking his hair softly and whispering loving words.

"Tell me how you made sex with the stupid American woman. Was she good?"

By bits and pieces, he started to tell her how this woman was madly in love with him. How she was starved for sex and willing to do anything.

"I had good time" he laughed sleepily, "but she was *stupido*."

"You keep saying that. Why was she so stupid?" asked Monica, continuing to stroke and caress him.

"She bought boat for me, *barca bellissimo*!" And he proceeded to tell her that this woman insisted on taking the boat into open waters, even though they were warned for heavy winds. She didn't want to sit down and tried to take over the wheel.

Mario was by now more sleepy than sexy, his head flopped, but Monica kissed him and said:

"What happened then?"

"*Alora* accident" he mumbled, his English becoming worse, "*barca incidente mortala*, Esther dead." Tears ran over his cheeks.

"Oh, my poor Mario, you must have loved her."

That woke him up a bit:

"*Non vero!*" Again, he declared that she was a *donna stupida*.

"*Mama mia, barca Mario!*"

In his broken English, he proceeded to tell her about the things he loved about the boat: the two Johnson outboard motors, the teak timber deck, a galley, and a love nest. She understood the tears were for the boat he lost and not for his lover. After his outburst of grief, his eyes dropped again while he snuggled against her. She returned to stroking his hair while trying to get more information out of him:

"How do you know she was dead?"

"*Non, non ha permesso* to tell. *Polizia!*"

But he still continued mumbling. Listening carefully, she could make out that the police obviously threatened him with jail. They wanted to avoid an international scandal and had her buried as a nameless prostitute!

She kept saying soothing words to him, till big, strong, sexy Mario was fast asleep. She looked at the handsome gondolier with some regret. She had hated doing what she did, but saw no other way to get information out of him. Leaving him an envelope with money to cover his time, she dressed quickly. By now it was nearly midnight, but Italy never sleeps and a bright-eyed clerk at the lobby took her payment for the room without question and called a gondolier to bring her back to her hotel.

Not wanting to give Mario a chance to find her, she had a shower, changed into a comfortable outfit for travelling and booked out as soon as she was packed. Even in the middle of the night it was no problem to find transport to the airport where she waited for the first available seat to anywhere.

The earliest flight out was to Frankfurt and she managed to get a seat on it while she also booked a business class ticket to go from there to New York. After getting rid of her suitcase, she made herself as comfortable as possible for the long wait, as the VIP lounge had closed.

She used the time to update her social pages and check her mail. Eric had sent her a worried email. He was eagerly looking forward to hearing from her and made her curious by hinting about new developments where he needed her input.

She responded that she was waiting for a flight, but had to take a detour via Frankfurt. She was OK and keen to update him on what she had found out, but did not want to put it in an email. She would be arriving at McGhee Tyson Airport just before 6 p.m. after a 16-hour flight from Frankfurt via Washington, and hoped somebody would pick her up from there. "It's lucky that my doctor gave me something to help me sleep on the plane", she wrote. "Very much looking forward to see you."

-.-.-.-

CHAPTER 7

During the fortnight that Monica was away, things had been happening in Castleburg. Professor Sebastian had returned for a short visit to the Sacksenheimer Estate and brought news from Boston.

"Remember our discussion about supercomputers?" he asked Eric.

"Well, Harvard University bought one not that long ago. They cannot afford to run it anymore and the power supply, like everywhere, is unpredictable. The government funding has been cut back so much that they must lay off staff and are only increasing student intake with students from overseas countries as they can charge them exorbitant fees. They are struggling and trying to sell the supercomputer. It's a late model Cray." Eric's eyes lit up.

"A supercomputer! For sale! Any idea what they want for it?"

"Don't know, but I do know that they paid well over twenty million for it."

"Holy mackerel! Who should I speak to?" Eric queried., "Not that I am prepared to pay that much", he murmured more to himself than to Sebastian who picked it up anyway and responded,

"If you are serious, contact the senior vice-president, Dr Gene Roberts. He oversees all finances. They might be happy to consider a much lower offer as they need the cash and do not have any offers yet as far as I understand."

"I will definitely consider it and see what I can learn about the Cray computer."

Eric went in search of Anthony who exploded with enthusiasm.

"A supercomputer! Fantastic! Are you going to buy it? Really? What kind is it? A Cray you say? With no liquid cooling? That will save you! Will I be allowed to work with it?"

"Calm down, Anthony" Eric laughed. "We do not own it yet. I wish Monica was here with her legal and computer knowledge, but you can probably help just as well. I am planning to accompany the professor when he returns to Boston the day after tomorrow. We are trying to get an appointment to see the university's financial manager. We will see what comes of it. I have read and learned a bit about what supercomputers can do, but have no real understanding of how it all works nor does the professor. We need you to write down the most important things we need to get information about. For instance: how do we prepare for installation, what are the power needs, etc. I am sure you will come up with many questions. Go for it."

"I will do some research and get back to you" Anthony said, containing his urge to make a few somersaults.

Armed with a list of questions, Eric and Sebastian set off for Boston where they had a constructive meeting with Dr Roberts who called the computer's technician in to answer all the questions that Anthony had carefully prepared. The meeting was concluded by Eric's offer of 15 million, including permission for the technician, if he was willing, to accompany the computer and relocate to Castleburg. Dr Roberts promised to put it to the Board at the next meeting.

The professor went back to work and Eric went to the airport for the next flight back home. During the flight, he checked his e-mails and read that Monica's plane would be landing only two hours after him. He decided to wait for her; looking forward to the hour-long drive they would share. He had grown very fond of her and had missed her company.

Monica was very surprised to find Eric waiting for her and didn't try to hide her pleasure. She spontaneously hugged him and put her arm through his while waiting for her suitcase. The drive was spent updating each other on the happenings on either side of the globe. Monica said that she thought Europe also was struggling but coping a bit better with the economic problems. She didn't pick up a feeling of doom, like she felt sometimes in their own country. She had been a tourist of course, on a very short visit. Apart from continuing huge refugee problems and some demonstrations, she did not experience a lot of unrest or upheaval.

The tourist industry was struggling a bit; hotels did not have many guests and she saw lots of advertising for holiday deals.

"Tell me how you went with Ben Homer. I have not heard from him for a while."

"He is a useless man that likes his whiskey too much, and the only thing I learned from him is that the gondolier's name was Mario and that he could not locate him." Then she told Eric how she found Mario and what she learned, without revealing too much detail about her tactics. She was glad that they were driving and her face was hidden now the sun had gone down. Talking about it would have been much more difficult if he had been sitting opposite her and able to search her face. As a lawyer, she was very adept at hiding her feelings but this had become a bit personal.

"I am so sorry, Eric, but I am quite sure that Esther died in a motorboat accident the day she disappeared. It is shocking that you were not notified. It seemed that the police, possibly ordered by a higher authority afraid of an international scandal, threatened the gondolier with jail and told him to keep his mouth shut. If anybody asked, he had to deny that he was the Mario that steered the motorboat. They had her buried as an unknown prostitute in a common grave. I am really, really sorry to have to tell you that."

Eric stayed silent for a while, pondering the information.

"I am so grateful to you for finally confirming what I already suspected, that Esther is dead. It will be especially sad for her parents who also stopped hearing from her at the same time. I will call Esther's brother who I get on well with and relate the news. They might take it further but for me, the case is closed now, except that I will tell Homer to find out where they would have buried an unidentified body thought to be a prostitute. He can then send me a final report, which I will forward to Esther's family."

Then, wanting to change to a happier subject, he asked her about the wedding she attended. With enthusiasm, she described the three-day wedding in a medieval castle located in the beautiful, sunny, and peaceful countryside outside of Florence. She told about the joyous atmosphere during the ceremony. There had been several celebrations afterwards with different groups of people, and also been plenty of time for sunning in the gardens, exercising her limited Italian and getting to know her friend's new husband a bit. Very conveniently, she was provided with luxurious accommodation at the castle together with other close friends and family members. She added: "I can tell you Tuscany is a beautiful part of Italy and Rome is spectacular with monuments on every street corner and so much history! I took lots of photos to show you later."

Both now in a more cheerful mood, Monica said,

"And now it's your turn. You have made me very curious with your e-mail. Why do you need my input, and for what?" As they were already close to Castleburg, Eric said:

"I know a small restaurant nearby with a great reputation. Can I tempt you with dinner so that we can continue talking? I am so happy to see you back and safe; I would like to postpone sharing you with others."

Although quite tired after nearly 24 hour travelling and not very hungry, she accepted his invitation gladly, not wanting to end their time together either. While enjoying a lovely meal, and sharing a bottle of wine, Eric told her about the development of the last few days and the offer he had made for the supercomputer.

"If I had known you were on your way back, I would have postponed that meeting for a day as we could have done with your expertise. But as it is, Anthony helped us out with a list of questions. I have it here."

He produced the list, now with answers as well, from the inside pocket of his jacket. Handing it to her, he added:

"Do not worry about it today, just keep it with you and have a think about it when you are rested. I think the university's board of directors will have a meeting tomorrow. We probably will not get a response till a few days after. And we still can get out of it if we want."

Remembering that they talked about supercomputers but a bit puzzled about Eric's reasons for spending that much money, she put the notes away to think about it later.

Eric proceeded to tell her about other developments since her departure. The power connection to the house had been completed. And finally, the change to his production line was now fully operational with the help of Anthony who programmed the factory computer expertly. Cutting out the expensive soaps in solid as well as liquid forms saved them an enormous amount of power. Talking about going back to the original, simple soaps led them to talk about Eric's parents and his youth. He told Monica that he had a very privileged upbringing.

He attended private boarding schools while spending his holidays on their property and in and around the factory that had been started by his grandfather before he was born. "My grandfather looked a bit like Sebastian", Eric smiled nostalgically. "And I loved him very much."

"However, I did not make my family very proud during my adolescence." he admitted sheepishly. "I got in with the wrong crowd and thought life was all about having a good time and making lots of money! I came to my senses when my mum fell seriously ill with breast cancer."

He told Monica that he studied then very hard and managed to do his final exams well enough to gain entry to his preferred course at university and make his mum proud.

After initially getting better, his mother's illness returned shortly after Eric graduated as a chemical engineer. This time it was fatal.

"Soon after, my grandfather unexpectedly died too from a massive heart attack. Dad and I tried to bury our sadness into hard work and I was glad to be able to help dad bring his idea of becoming self-sufficient into practice. At least we started on it, but then his health deteriorated and he needed open heart surgery. After that, he had to cut down on work and talked me into finding a mate. I was seeing Esther at the time and was in love with her beauty, so we married. I think dad had a good influence on her and the first few years, we were quite happy. Oh well, I told you the rest before."

"The last of dad's ideas have now been completed and I am confident we will generate a lot of energy, more than enough for this supercomputer as well."

Continuing to update Monica, Eric told her that the old-fashioned wood stove had been removed from the kitchen. Pam was out of her depth trying to work with the electrical appliances and her unhappiness was showing in the declining quality of her cooking. Everybody was looking forward to the arrival of Chris to take over.

With Anthony having his meals in the kitchen, Sebastian back to Boston and Monica away, life had become quite lonely again, Eric said. He missed their company and the lively discussions they had. Holding Monica's gaze for a moment, he wanted to say more but hesitated too long and the moment passed.

"Just as well", he thought later, not being sure of her reaction. He didn't want to jeopardize the relationship as it was now.

The next afternoon, Eric received a call from Dr Roberts telling him that the board would accept $16 million and that the technician was prepared to relocate to Castleburg if his salary was guaranteed.

Eric accepted the price and replied that he just needed one final meeting with his team before being able to give a definite yes or no.

The three of them sat together till late in the night. Eric told them how Anthony's casual remark about a supercomputer governing the country set his thoughts flying. When Sebastian told him about this computer, he made up his mind to commit to experiment with the capabilities and possibilities of a supercomputer. That is, if he could persuade them to commit as well.

He already talked to Sebastian and convinced him to be part of it. Their meetings would need the contribution of his valuable insights into society's workings. Maybe he would even quit Harvard and become a free-lance lecturer.

They would have to form a board of management and formulate an official agreement between them. Eric would guarantee them a basic salary until they agreed that the experiment had come to an end. The technician that would come with the computer would be employed by Eric and would, just as his factory's technician, be involved with the team, but not part of the board.

"Look" Eric said, "I am the last in my line. I inherited and added to a substantial fortune. I am prepared to gamble a big part of that on this experiment. If we can discover a way to change the fortunes of this country, I think it will be worth it."

He got them fired up and before retiring for the night, Monica and Anthony gave him their full commitment to the experiment.

The deal about the supercomputer was finalized. Eric received the assurance that only confidential information would be deleted. It meant they would be able to start their experiment using the results of many researches. For instance, research on decisions made by past governments, on scientific topics, statistics compiled from masses of data, like last year's census, and others.

The supercomputer's technician, Danny Lambert, arrived a few days later to prepare for the computer's instalment. Danny's age was difficult to guess; he could be 35, but just as well in his fifties; a tiny, balding, intense man with piercing eyes behind thick glasses. He found temporary accommodation with the help of the factory's engineer. This engineer, by the name of Jonathan Smith, was very different to Danny in appearance: a middle aged, black man of medium height with a friendly face topped by a head of curly, greying hair.

Eric was relieved to notice, already during the first meeting, that they got on well, each respectful of the other's expertise.

This meeting, more a discussion while walking through the factory, was about where and how to install the supercomputer. It was decided that the computer would be housed in a large but unused factory hall. They would have to build special housing for it.

Eric drew a basic sketch, which showed a miniature copy of the Congress Hall of the USA Government, with access to the supercomputer on the central table, and at least three half- round tiers of benches. Each seat would be provided with a microphone. Three big screens on the walls to allow everybody to follow the proceedings.

As it was intended to be an experiment and not a permanent fixture in the factory, Eric told them to put in a floating floor to hide all cabling and ducting. He expected to have plenty of space to store the bulkier parts of the computer under the tiers of the benches. He left it to Danny and Jonathan to discuss the changes with his building contractor, including the air-conditioned cooling system and insulation.

He was relieved that he did not have to install a liquid cooling system. It would save him quite some money. This kind of computer required less power. The two experts had to work out if the power supply would be sufficient, as expected, or whether they would have to find other solutions.

Sebastian called to report that, now the university was downsizing, it was very likely that they would not renew his contract when it was due at the end of the month. He was happy to accept Eric's offer and keen to be involved, although he still had some reservations about the feasibility of the project.

Danny Lambert was invited when the whole team, including the professor, was present for their first meeting. He explained that the supercomputer worked differently from other computers and much more efficiently because it could handle multiple inputs at the same time, rather than the sequential processing of the classic computers.

The supercomputer would then independently process and organise the received data, after which it would deliver a report. The ability of the computer was so advanced that, if it was programmed well, it would not deliver a final report if the data was not sufficient, even detailing the kind of data that was still needed.

With the help of Monica and Anthony who could translate most of the technical stuff into layman's terms, even Eric and Sebastian gained a basic understanding of the supercomputer's technical workings.

"It is fortunate" Danny said, "that during the last two years, the computer has been used extensively by several departments. Of course, classified information has been wiped but all information gathered and freely accessible to students and teachers has been left on.

"As you told me" he said, looking at Eric, "about the experiment you are planning, you might especially be interested in records and statistics gathered from all Congress meetings and from published research that was ordered by the different departments of government over the last several years."

Sebastian who had been quiet during the technical explanation said: "That information will be very valuable to us. Thank you, Danny."

-.-.-.-

CHAPTER 8

Their meeting continued after Danny excused himself to attend to the preparations for the computer's as well as his own relocation.

Sebastian cautioned that before going into politics, they needed to have many discussions.

"We need to be in full agreement about the basic premises we are talking from," he said giving some samples.: "We may have to agree if we are for or against the death penalty, for or against gun control. We may need to decide if we want to improve the economy by sticking with the basic capitalist principles this country is built on, or go for more socialist or even communist principles in relation to the distribution of wealth, or seek some combination. Are we only looking for solutions for our country and what could be the consequences of that internationally? If we become too myopic, we might start leaning towards national socialism or even fascism, we might find international opposition and endanger in and export markets.

There is a lot to be considered before we discuss the kind of information we will feed to the supercomputer!"

Monica cautioned,

"When we consider all that, we have to remember that we are citizens of the USA and all decisions have to fall within the laws of this country."

"Hear, hear, the lawyer speaks! And Monica is right of course", Sebastian agreed. "You keep us on the right path, girl as we are trying to find solutions. Those solutions could have consequences for more nations than just our own."

Conscious of being the youngest, Anthony needed to summon up courage to say something but the subject was close to his heart. He said,

"To follow up on what the professor said, when we have fixed the economy but have in the meantime stuffed up the environment, what have we achieved?"

Eric replied,

"We wouldn't have achieved a lot, would we? But in principle, I think, it would be impossible to have fixed the economy and not at the same time to have looked after the environment. That would truly lead to a failed economy.

However, let's not get bogged down on detailed solutions. I think, as Sebastian suggested, we should consider the bigger picture more and decide from what premise we start thinking about the problems the government must find solutions for. Maybe we can ask the computer to help us find this premise by asking it to find the common ground of all the principles people have been living by in this country. I am thinking of principles derived from the different religions, from philosophy, from humanism, from the Bill of Rights, the constitution and so on."

"Careful" Sebastian interjected. "We have to use caution when asking the computer about religion. Each one of us has the freedom to believe whatever they want, but a computer cannot 'believe' or evaluate 'values' it only deals with facts."

"The professor is right" agreed Eric, "but that does not make it easier. We should agree on the basic principles to govern from. Maybe if we list the rules, rules to live by that are taught by all these belief systems. The computer might then be able to name principles that are shared by all or most and then maybe we will have a starting point. We will have to go over this many times, but, I hope you agree, it should be enough for today. Let's break up this meeting; so much to think about! Next week, same time, same place!"

Inspired, the whole team started to work, and to work hard.

Jonathan made sure that the building work would be finished in time, and Danny travelled between the university and the factory to make sure all the computer components were safely dismantled and transported to the new site. When the supercomputer finally arrived, Danny, in close collaboration with Jonathan, oversaw the installation.

They had prepared well: the power connections were ready, the storage adequately insulated, the air-conditioned cooling system worked well. When all was done and thoroughly checked, Danny gave a demonstration to Monica and Anthony of how to access the data already stored, and how to load new information and programs. Paying close attention, they only now started to realise what this computer could do. It was indeed "super"!

Between the weekly meetings, everybody was very busy. Monica and Anthony continued to write down ideas for programming, while Sebastian was researching and formulating principles for a good system of government.

Eric, in the meantime, had to run the factory but was constantly mulling over the big questions. One day, when he was busy paying the flood of bills, he was caught by surprise when Monica knocked on his office door and offered that, if necessary, she could help with the cash flow.

"That is a great offer", Eric said hesitantly. "But then we have to make a decent contract."

Monica laughed,

"Remember? I am a lawyer! I will make sure to get my money back. But joking aside, it is a good idea. I will write a contract we can both sign if you agree with it."

After they agreed about the terms and conditions, Eric said,

"Let me know when you have it ready and I will take you out one night to celebrate. I like having a partner!"

The professor found it most difficult to try to formulate a common ground on which to base everything. He was highly qualified in political philosophy, but philosophy is more a science of asking questions than of giving answers. When Eric asked him how he was going, he shook his head:

"You know" he said, "what is certain today is often challenged or even disproved tomorrow. The rules we are looking for have to be of a general nature." They sat together thinking of how to accomplish what they intended to do.

"Look" Sebastian said, "if that computer is so clever, maybe we can feed it a lot of history, not only from our country, but also from those countries that seem to do better than us. You know, like what decisions were made under what kind of circumstances and with what kind of outcomes."

"Yes, yes," Eric said encouragingly, "keep going my friend."

"As you said before, Eric, we could also feed it things like the guidelines we find in Christianity, Islam, Hinduism, Buddhism, Humanism, as well as the US Constitution and Bill of Rights to help us find common guidelines that will appeal to us all. The good thing is that a computer is impartial and its conclusions cannot be based on greed, racism, or discrimination on any grounds."

Sebastian sighed deeply,

"It keeps escaping me how to decide from what premises we should start. We need to keep thinking and discussing those things often. I am lecturing now, but have I told you that Socrates already thought a lot about how to organise society best? In his teachings, he tried to consider the whole human being, his economic and social status as well as his temperament. The Greeks have given us a clear sample of good government, but it can of course only be seen in the light of their own time and circumstances. Today, things are different and much more complex. Instead of a 'city-state', we are speaking of hundreds of millions of people living in states, cities and villages, that are often divided among themselves, not even considering the whole world. The problems of today that are caused by global warming are among the biggest problems we must deal with.

"If we are ever to succeed in getting our president interested enough to listen, we will only be able to show a basic example of how the computer could serve the government. They will need more expertise, for instance: in economics, the environment, defence, etc. These experts should be trusted people, appointed by the president, and they will have to underwrite the principles we are trying to formulate now."

And on and on the talks went. Every weekend, they had their meeting and, unusual for meetings, all participants were looking forward to them, always again surprised with and excited about the ideas that came up for discussion and the progress they made.

They talked about possibly changing the way a president was elected and if and how donations to campaigns should be regulated. They agreed that the present situation was not very democratic. At present, a candidate would have to spend huge amounts of money on publicity to have any chance of being elected. That money would usually be a large part of their own money, so very rich people had the best chances. Apart from their own money, companies and/or individuals donated enormous amounts of money with the consequence that they expected favours in return. Not democratic at all!

Their meetings always started with a lecture from the professor, as more insights gained from 'political philosophy' would help them to build the framework they were all working on. These lectures were often very deep and a new experience for this audience. Even though they were all educated and had attended university, for people used to the exact sciences of engineering and computers, and even to law with its precise descriptions, the professor was not always easy to follow.

He apologised for that and explained that to put thoughts into words is basically flawed as our command of the language is often not adequate, and he understood that for people not schooled in philosophy, it would be difficult sometimes. He took as example what had happened to the science of climate change. Scientists, so used to speaking to students and fellow academics, had difficulty explaining the changing environment to the public, resulting in people dismissing the science that threatened to change their way of life, especially when other people that spoke their language argued against it.

However, over time, Sebastian got better in explaining the philosophic look at politics, the questions it gave birth to, and how it could help them develop a new and positive view of politics. They asked him to write down his lectures so they could study them later, but Eric saved him that work by buying a dicta-phone and had the lectures transcribed and distributed.

At one of these meetings, the professor told them about a parable called 'The Tragedy of the Commons', an economic theory, written in 1833 by William Foster Lloyd.

"The story is broadly as follows: It tells about a group of herders and their families. They each owned a flock of animals and shared the use of a piece of land called "the Commons", large enough to support many animals. Some herders decided to breed more animals to expand their flock and gained a substantial benefit when selling them at the market. However, the cost of maintaining the animals, the common land and water, is shared by all; so, he who gains a lot but pays little will be encouraged to keep adding to his flock. Of course, every other herder wants to do the same and they all add to their fortune until the Common becomes a wasteland and is not able to support any animals.

Then the whole tribe starves."

"This parable highlights the problem of co-operation. We should find a solution to that problem and make collective interest win over individual interest. This is "the central problem of social co-existence.""

At the moment, we can see our 'common' world fast becoming incapable of supporting its inhabitants. We can also see many cases of people benefiting as an individual from their ability to deny the truth, even though society of which they are a part, suffers. Think: wars, climate change, slave labour, etc."

"We need to open people's eyes and encourage them to become 'herders', putting *us*' ahead of '*me*' and so prevent the "tragedy of the commons" from happening."

Then Sebastian used the team itself as example:

"None of you could have accomplished individually what we have created together so far. Co-operation between people, different minds, ideas, capabilities, is essential for finding solutions to complicated matters."

"True! You are right as usual, Uncle Sebastian" Monica said, "but how can the supercomputer make people in government co-operate better? Will it be possible to make a persuasive program about that?"

They kept talking about it for a long time but did not come up with any satisfactory answers, and the strain was starting to show. On top of that, there were some technical problems: Danny was struggling with the speaker's desk. The speaker had to have a control centre with its own computer screen. He ended up providing three screens and a keyboard that could override all before being satisfied.

Eric made them all, including Danny, take the weekend off to recharge the batteries and took them out hiking in the Great Smoky Mountain National Park. It was a real bonding experience. Although the professor excused himself from the most strenuous hike, he enjoyed, just like the others, the fresh mountain air and the companionship.

Refreshed, they took up their task with renewed energy. Inspired by the "*Tragedy of the Commons*" they gathered new data during weeks and months of hard work and meetings, which they fed into the supercomputer.

Finally, they had progressed to a point where Anthony could load the new program he and Monica had created. Now it was possible to order the computer to draw conclusions based on the old and new data available.

They were looking forward to have a test run.

-.-.-.-

CHAPTER 9

The team assembled in the factory hall that had now been adapted to resemble a meeting room for Congress at the Capitol.

Eric took the microphone and said,

"As the Secretary for Energy, I propose to invest $100 million in exploring new oil reserves that were discovered in the Antarctic."

The supercomputer took only a few seconds to come back with a negative response based on detailed data from several researches into the feasibility of this plan compared with other feasibility research of investments in renewable industry, including the cost to the environment and the opportunities for employment of both plans.

The four of them erupted into enthusiastic applause.

"That is it!" Eric exclaimed. "That's what we want to show the president. It will cut out so much time spent on useless discussions about so- called facts that are often disproved later. And don't forget the time and energy spent nowadays on all kind of committees and inquiries. This computer could come to conclusions in a fraction of the time. If the supercomputer is kept up-to-date with all available data, then there won't be any arguing with its conclusions."

After many test runs, their very ambitious plan was to invite President Brown, plus as many members of Congress as were willing, to travel to Castleburg for a demonstration and then count on the persuasive powers of President Brown to convince the government to give permission to buy the supercomputer.

Eric travelled to Washington to present their case. Through his connections in high places, he had managed to secure a 15-minute interview with the president. Despite these connections, he had to come a day early to go through a tough security check at the Secret Service office. He had to show and leave copies of all his identity papers and underwent two interviews with different officers.

Relieved that was over, he looked forward to a relaxing dinner and evening with Monica who had agreed to join him for a night out in Washington to finally celebrate the signing of the contract between them, as he had promised. He didn't feel the need to prepare for the next day. After so many months of thinking and talking and trials, he knew exactly what he was going to say and was confident to have answers for any questions the president could throw at him. So, he had booked tickets for the opera. They were performing his favourite opera, "La Bohème". He never asked her but was confident that Monica would like this opera too.

Before the show, they enjoyed a delicious dinner at a restaurant nearby. He asked her about her family and interests besides her studies. Affected by the lovely atmosphere in the restaurant and the euphoria about the results of their hard work, she opened up and told him about a happy, carefree youth, her love of reading and playing hockey. She played hockey till a few years ago, when an unlucky encounter with a hockey ball dislocated her shoulder. She took the advice of her doctor and stopped playing. She told of the devastation of her mother, her sister and herself on losing the man they loved so much so suddenly. Her mother lived for a while with her in the hotel, but everything reminded her of her loss and she packed up and moved to California, close to Monica's sister, son-in-law and three grandchildren.

"Thanks for sharing that with me" Eric said, "you went through some difficult times."

They ate in companionly silence for a bit, broken by Eric a bit later,

"Now, tell me about something else. You know everything about my disastrous marriage, what about you? Have you been in love?" Laughingly Monica said:

"Yes, of course I have. Too many times! But it never lasted long. I usually found that I was more interested in what I was doing than in a commitment to a relationship. So, I suppose I have not been really 'in love'."

Monica had never been to an opera before and she laughed and cried and sought his hand during the sad scenes towards the end of the story.

Feeling close, they didn't let go of each other on the way to the hotel. Eric had booked separate rooms, but arriving at his room he said: "Come in please, I don't want to say goodnight yet, let's have a glass of wine together."

Inside, he pulled her into his arms and kissed her deeply. To his relief, Monica responded passionately and they forgot about the wine. The night became a celebration of the feelings that had been building up between them from the first time they met.

Monica was still sleeping when Eric left for his interview with the president. He left her a note saying that he loved her and to wait for him so they could travel back together.

Only on arriving at the White House, he was informed that he had security clearance. However, he still had to go through security screens before being allowed into the waiting room of the Oval Office. While he was admiring a beautiful painting of a three-master sailing ship on a wild ocean, the personal secretary of the president came in and opened the door to the office announcing the visitor to President Brown. Looking up from his desk and appearing much older than on television, the president welcomed him with the words:

"You have me intrigued with your letter, Mr. von Sacksenheim., Please sit down and tell me more about it."

"Thank you, Mr. President., I appreciate this interview very much." Eric responded and proceeded to explain that he had formed a team with very capable and trusted people: esteemed professor Sebastian Bergsteyn, his niece, lawyer, and computer scientist Monica Bergsteyn, computer programmer Anthony Sanders and himself, owner of the multi-million-dollar business, "Sacksenheimer Soaps" in Castleburg, Tennessee.

He emphasised how concerned the four of them were about the country's situation, especially Eric himself, after his eye-opening visit to the City of New York where parts of the city were not safe anymore. Many people had lost their employment and their home. Consequently, there was a lot of crime, police not coping, and people barricading their houses. The same situation was spreading into the suburbs and country towns.

"With apologies, Mr President" Eric said, "the four of us agreed that we had lost confidence in our government and one of us thought a supercomputer might be able to help get our rulers out of the rut they seem to be in."

"This is the part I didn't understand in your request for an interview, but I am surely intrigued," remarked the president, ignoring the criticism.

Eric explained then how far they had come. They still had a long way to go but would soon be ready to give a demonstration to a good proportion of the government, including the opposition, if the president would be interested.

President Brown and Eric then talked about how most politicians initially went into politics because they wanted to make a difference, to improve life for all Americans. Of course, they came from different perspectives with different backgrounds, but a good government should be able to find a middle way. Eric recounted some of the discussions he had with his team.

"We think that most problems are caused because many of those politicians that started out with good intentions, slowly got corrupted by the influence, persuasion, and money of big business, organisations or people in power, by being forced to toe the party-line and by getting power-hungry themselves. This is something a computer cannot change by itself, but now" Eric argued, "is the time when indisputable facts, convincingly shown by the supercomputer, could change attitudes." They agreed that most politicians were desperate and looking for real solutions. There would probably still be the odd politician that still believed that the markets would always correct themselves in time. His team expected that they would now be only a small minority.

Eric stressed that it would be most important that the computer would be kept up-to-date with all research, so politicians could be confident to make good decisions with the help of information based on the latest, independent data. Information presented by the computer and trusted to be free of any bias would save them a lot of time. Time that all politicians, being the representatives of the people, would be able to spend with their constituents and so become better informed of where the need for governing lay, and why and where to initiate research in which areas. It would also make for a much happier politician and for much more inspired debate in the White House and at Capitol Hill.

"We have dedicated a part of my factory to function as a demonstration room that can hold more than a hundred people. If you are interested, I hope it will be possible to keep it secret for the time being, so it won't be torpedoed beforehand."

For a long while, the president was silent. Eric waited patiently. Finally, he looked up and said,

"I might be interested, Mr. von Sacksenheim. Thank you very much for bringing this innovative idea to my attention. I will talk it over with the vice-president and my chief of staff. You will be contacted if we want to take this any further."

With these words, Eric was dismissed. Even though no definite approval for a test had been given, he was nevertheless very happy with the visit and looked forward to tell Monica about it.

But that was not to be. Monica had left the hotel. When he paid the bill, he was handed a note from her saying that she was sorry but 'I bumped into a study-mate from long ago here in the lobby. She is in town for a conference but had time to spare today. I don't want to lose the opportunity to catch up so decided to stay another night and travel back tomorrow. I also enjoyed the night, no regrets!' The note continued, 'But please Eric, let's take it slow. It might work out between us or it might not. I don't want to run the risk of ruining our co-operation at this stage. OK? XO Monica.'

"Well, at least, she left me a kiss and a hug", Eric thought, "I"ll be patient."

-.-.-.-

CHAPTER 10

Eric's team was impressed with his report of the visit. They decided to act as if there would be an official test soon and redoubled their efforts to prepare for a trial run and make it as fail proof as they possibly could.

Two weeks passed and then, unannounced, just when they were having their Saturday meeting, a six- men security team turned up. They insisted on having access to everything, the whole factory, the offices, the surrounding grounds and particularly, the demonstration room.

They took lots of photos, including from every person present while demanding proof of identity. In addition to the security team, there was also a computer expert—he was not as knowledgeable as Danny Lambert, but enough to be mightily impressed with the capabilities of the supercomputer. The eighth person was a woman, Lisa Leatherman.

She turned out to be the right-hand of the secretary of state, an attractive middle-aged woman, stylish, very businesslike but friendly. She made them feel comfortable while she interviewed every member of the team.

When they were ready to leave, Ms Leatherman explained that they would have to report to President Brown. If this would indeed lead to a visit from the president himself, the security team would inform them if there were changes to be made to improve security.

And then, on another Saturday morning a few weeks later, they got a call from the FBI that their helicopter would land shortly on the parking lot. They were told to prepare for a two- hour visit from the president and his chief of staff. The last visit had not found any security issues with the factory and offices but they would still have another test run before the president would be cleared to land. This started frantic preparations, as the team was keen to show off what the computer could do.

It turned out to be a top-secret visit as officially President Brown and his chief of staff were heading to Camp David, which they would do afterwards.

When the important visitors arrived, the team was in position. Eric and Danny showed them around. President Brown was a lot less formal than on the day Eric had his interview and treated Eric as an equal, even a friend. Eric explained how they would like as many politicians as possible from both parties to be seated behind the desks. In consultation with the president and his team, they would set a subject for discussion and then ask the politicians for comments and suggestions. They demonstrated the example of Eric posing as the secretary for energy wanting to invest in exploring new oil reserves in the Antarctic and made a convincing case. The president and his chief of staff were impressed and seemed confident to gain Cabinet's approval for Eric to stage a showcase of this new approach to governing the country. President Brown said he would be sending in a few trusted people from his team to collect all the details and consult with Eric's team to prepare a detailed plan and set a date. He would then be updated so he could present it to the government and prepare a speech to close off the demonstration.

When it was time to go, they walked together to the helicopter. Eric managed to get a private moment with the president.

"Mr President, I wonder if I could ask you a personal favour?"

"Feel free", said the president. "What is it?"

"Would it be possible and would you be willing to marry Monica Bergsteyn and me at the end of your next visit? Naturally, presumed that there will be a next visit. I have not officially asked her yet and would like it to be a total surprise."

"I think I could accommodate that", the president smiled. "It will be an interesting addition to my usual duties and definitely less stressful. Arrange everything with my secretary and make sure all legal requirements are met. I hope you are certain to get a positive response!" Happily, Eric replied that he was confident of Monica's 'yes' and assured him that all information would be supplied in time and there would be no legal hiccups.

Many weeks passed but finally, they got the news that the trial was approved and the date was set.

It was again a Saturday so the factory was closed. They were well prepared but still very anxious about what this day would bring. As expected, the first ones to arrive were the security people. After declaring the site safe, most of them kept out of sight except for the ones guarding the doors. Then, all fifteen cabinet members arrived by bus from Tyson Airport, followed by several buses filled with members of both houses. Everyone was a bit apprehensive as to the purpose of this visit, which had been kept secret. Why would the president have urged them to come to a soap factory and why were they ushered into a big hall that was set-up to look like the Congress Hall at Capitol Hill?

Only two journalists trusted by the government were invited under strict rules of secrecy until the president would be ready to address Congress.

Eric had to explain to the security people and to Monica why the local judge was invited to be present. He introduced him as a friend and somebody he consulted often and left it at that. His identity papers proving he was a judge were enough to give him security clearance.

When the president arrived by helicopter and everyone was seated, the speaker asked everybody to stand while Eric announced the entrance of the president. He performed that duty as if it was his daily task.

President Brown held a short speech in which he thanked the delegates and members of Congress, that they had made themselves available for this very important demonstration. He also thanked Eric and his dedicated team for all their hard work.

The speaker then asked Eric to please explain what the demonstration was all about. Eric stood up and thanked the president, the speaker and the audience before introducing his team.

"We had this dream that we could program a supercomputer in such a way that it would assist you, our government, to find solutions for the problems our country is facing." He continued to explain how the computer would work and how it would be able to save the government a lot of time and money.

"I think we all agree that harsh measures might have to be taken to get out of the impasse we are in. It is very important to be sure that those measures will have positive results. If the electorate sees good results, they will better support the government and make your job easier. We will first do a prepared test to show you how it works. After that, we will ask the speaker to conduct one of your normal sessions and demonstrate how the computer could be part of that."

Eric then asked the speaker to engage the computer with the help of Danny. Eric played his role as secretary for energy asking Congress to please approve $100 million for further oil exploration in the Antarctic. After Eric sat down, the Speaker asked the computer for comments and everyone could hear the response as the computer was on "speaker phone".

Like the president had heard before, the metallic voice commented, "that it would be, under the present circumstances, not advisable to approve that sum of money" and it explained the reasons with graphs and research results that everyone could follow on the three large screens.

About half the delegates gave a lukewarm applause, probably expecting that the answer had been set up.

However, they sat up and paid attention when the Speaker got to the order of the day and asked the member of Arkansas to please put his case forward as there was not enough time to discuss it during the last session.

The Representative from Arkansas stood up, and Anthony took care that the microphone was clearly picking up his voice. This man, proving to be a good orator, spoke convincingly about the need for a tunnel under the Mississippi to improve the infrastructure of his State. He argued that the $20 billion investment would be very good for the economy, supporting trades and creating a lot of employment while the improved infrastructure would bring more business and tourists to the area.

When he sat down, the Speaker of the house invited other representatives to give their point of view on the matter. The member representing Louisiana was given the chair. He described in very colourful language why the country could not afford such an extravagant expense. If Arkansas was so desperate for a tunnel, the State should fund it. After this speech, the Speaker asked the computer to give its comments.

In its metallic voice, the supercomputer answered,

"The first speaker spoke for 14-and-a-half minutes, which is 9and-half minutes too long and therefore will be fined 9-and-a-half times $50. He also used provocative language in sentence 64 and receives his first warning for overstepping the rules of the house." An audible gasp went through the audience.

"The second speaker spoke for nearly 13 minutes and is therefore fined 8 times $50. He used offensive, racist language in sentence 24 and 87, and is fined the set fine of $500 for each offence."

"The Representative for Arkansas argued strongly against the tunnel proposal one year ago, and has not explained why he changed his mind. Research from the University of Arkansas, supported by research of the Research Institute of Washington, has indicated that costs will blow out to at least 22 billion and the interest, considering the inflation forecast, will add an extra billion per year. Based on the mentioned research, the benefit to all users amounts to about 5% while the benefit to the citizens of the State cannot amount to more than 2.5%. This proposal should not be approved as the total return does not warrant the outlay of such a capital."

The assembly was flabbergasted. Many showed their approval and applauded the result.

When the applause died down, Monica got up and asked the Speaker to allow her to explain a bit more.

"The Chair is for Miss Bergsteyn", the Speaker said.

"I think it is appropriate to explain a bit about the rules of engagement we programmed into the computer", Monica said. "With apologies to the audience, our team came up with these rules after discussing the mistrust many people have in politicians. We must be honest and acknowledge that fact if we aim to get the public to support necessary but possibly unpopular measures the government will need to take to improve the economy. Most people are turned off by things like mudslinging, swearing, racist remarks and endless discussions that lead to nothing. They see it as a waste of time and a waste of their money. So, we have put in rules and fines for overstepping them as you have noticed. Of course, they are only examples and this program should be improved and extended by a joint government body of specialists covering all aspects of government. If you decide to go ahead, we suggest that you make this body independent of party-line politics. Thank you, Mr Speaker."

Monica sat down amid a generous applause, many people nodding their heads in agreement, including the president who had the Chair next.

"Ladies and Gentlemen, I hope you now understand the secrecy under which this meeting was organised. We won't be able to keep it a secret much longer" he said, looking in the direction of the two journalists, "but I ask for one day more. On Monday, Congress and Cabinet will have a joint sitting and make the decision to buy this supercomputer or not, and whether to commit to a different way of governing the country. If we decide to go ahead, and if the price is right . . ." and he looked questioningly at Eric who immediately responded with "Only 30 million, Mr. President." Which everybody heard and took notice of, but the president didn't particularly acknowledge the interjection and continued,

" . . . I will give a State of the Union address to the nation. I am confident that we will be able to muster more than sufficient support. I expect many, just like me, will be inspired by the real possibility of change. I suggest you all think deeply about the importance of your vote. And now, I hope you all join me in thanking Mr Eric von Sacksenheim and his team for the money, effort, and time they have invested in presenting us so convincingly with these results."

The team stood up and acknowledged the thundering applause that followed, beaming with pride.

Then the president motioned for Eric's team to keep standing.

"The helicopter is waiting for me. I won't stay for the refreshments that have been prepared for us, but I still have one very unusual task to complete before leaving. I have been asked that, if Miss Monica Bergsteyn is willing, and I surely hope so, to preside over the wedding ceremony between her and Mr Hans Eric von Sacksenheim. What will be your answer, Miss Bergsteyn?"

Monica, at first speechless and not believing her ears, came quickly to her senses, and shouted,

"Yes, yes, Mr President!" while looking with unbelief at Eric who had a big smile on his face.

Then she realised that she apparently was the only one of the team that was not informed, as Anthony produced a pillow with two rings, James presented her with a bouquet flowers straight from the garden, and her uncle and Danny stepped forward as witnesses. She understood then, too, why the local judge was present. He provided the legal requirements for President Brown to be able to conduct the ceremony. Before a smiling president, they promised to love and honour each other till death would them part.

While the surprised but happy audience rewarded them with another applause, the doors opened and tables full of delicious treats were wheeled into the hall. The President had to leave immediately, but most other people wanted to congratulate the happy couple and lingered over drinks, talking animatedly about the experiences of the day.

When they were finally alone, Monica pretended to be terribly upset:

"How could you do this to me? I will never forgive you for causing me to marry you in a business suit!"

"Wait till we are on our honeymoon", Eric teased. "Then you will wear much less! But seriously, you made me unbelievably happy by saying 'Yes'. Let's have a second wedding with family and friends, and you in a beautiful dress. Tell me the most important thing: are you happy?"

"Oh, yes!" Monica beamed.

-.-.-.-

CHAPTER 11

They gathered together in front of the television to watch the "State of the Union" address by the president. They fully realised then that the government would most probably buy the supercomputer, and James was called to bring in the champagne. In a euphoric mood, they listened to President Charles Brown, who gave an inspiring speech that was obviously meant to motivate all Americans to get behind the change and give their trust once more to their president, his cabinet, and their representatives to make the right decisions for the country.

Indeed, after the broadcast, Eric received a call from the president's office informing him that the government would buy the computer lock, stock, and barrel for the mentioned price of $30 million.

Their celebrations lasted till late in the night, especially when Eric announced a $100,000 bonus for every team member.

Sometime during the next week, a specialist team was chosen by the president and endorsed by the major parties. They would manage the computer in all aspects. As their position had to be above suspicion, they had to be willing to undergo extensive security checks followed by regular interviews.

Eric had been smart enough to inform his personnel on the day the secret was out. They were all watching the President's address in the computer room. Eric made them share his good luck by awarding them an extra week holiday on full pay while the business had to be closed for the transition. He told them not to talk to journalists, except to promote the town and tell local stories. Questions about the computer should be referred to him. He expected the media to make an appearance soon, and indeed, within hours of the president's speech, Castleburg was swamped with journalists of every persuasion.

At the start of the planned weeklong closure, the specialist team arrived in Castleburg and stayed the whole week as guests at the Sacksenheimer Estate. They were to receive practical instructions and attend several meetings with Eric's team and Danny Lambert, who had agreed to move to Washington with the supercomputer.

Eric's team enjoyed the interaction with these newcomers and shared the insights they had gained. Many lively discussions took place during dinnertime when everybody gathered together. The delicious dishes, prepared by Chris, added to a happy and positive atmosphere.

Danny was content that he would be able to keep looking after his 'baby', but a bit sad about leaving the team and the new friends he had made. Eric and Monica organised a special farewell night for Danny at the factory with all staff present. Danny was very well liked by everybody he met in the course of his work. He got a bit emotional when Jonathan spoke about how he not only admired Danny's expertise but enjoyed his friendship and would miss his companionship. Eric presented him with a beautiful picture of the factory, signed by everybody with 'good luck' messages and an envelope containing a generous bonus.

Soon, they started to move the supercomputer to the Capitol building in Washington. It took a bit of time to complete. They placed it, similarly to the factory hall, but with substantial adjustments, in the Chamber of the House of Representatives. Luckily, here they also found plenty of space underneath the tiered seating.

The team of specialists used the installation time to prepare for its first day of operation. They worked day and night and the result was spectacular.

From that first day on, it worked out as Eric's team planned and hoped for. Here and there something misfired, but overall, good decisions were made and implemented while much less time was wasted.

Although initially sceptical, people became increasingly motivated to support decisions of the government, helped by the fact that the televised sittings of parliament became more civilised and the representatives spent more time in their own states, meeting constituents, explaining policies and leading by example.

The overall mood of hopelessness in the country slowly changed and people started to help each other and support government programs to tackle homelessness and widespread poverty. Initiatives to clean up and improve the environment were taken, and slowly but surely cities became safer and cleaner, which made businesses that had closed return and provide more opportunities for employment.

It did not happen overnight, but success stories gave birth to more success stories. Even small positive steps to improve a situation inspired people to follow suit.

The world started to take notice. Politicians and authorities from other countries sent delegates or came over themselves to find out how the USA managed to turn back from the abyss.

During this period, life had returned to a kind of normal at the Sacksenheimer Estate. However, it still was not an ideal time for Monica and Eric to start their marriage and find some private time. Their minds were still busy going over everything they did and experienced, and the resulting changes that were starting to show all over the country. The professor and Anthony were similarly affected. All four still felt the need to talk about it to help them process their experiences. They had been on a very high stress level for a long time.

Because of this, Sebastian suggested to continue the regular meetings for a while, just to encourage them to off-load their feelings. With a few lessons in philosophy, he managed to put their experiences in perspective and they were all able to return their attention to the work they should be doing.

Anthony jumped on his bike every morning to attend to the factory's computers, perfecting the programs to improve production. In his spare time, he enjoyed helping Pam, who had returned from her holiday, with the vegetable garden and assisted wherever he was needed.

Professor Bergsteyn returned to his studies and research, lamenting that he would have liked the supercomputer to assist him. He took on more guest lectures and was thinking about doing a PhD in Philosophy of Computer Science for which he now had a lot of material.

Eric and Monica were relieved to finally have more time for themselves, but they mostly wanted to get away for a while. Eric could not do that just yet as he had neglected his business a bit, but he thought a couple of months of hard work would enable him to take some time off. He had great confidence in his staff to manage without him.

He encouraged Monica to use that time to organise their dream wedding. They agreed that it would not be a huge one, just a happy day with family and friends. The date was set, after which they would finally go on their honeymoon.

-.-.-.-

CHAPTER 12

On the day the wedding invitations were ready to be sent, an official looking envelope addressed to Mr and Mrs von Sacksenheim arrived by special delivery.

It turned out to be an invitation from the Secretary General of the United Nations, Dr François Vigneron, to join him for an informal afternoon tea in his personal offices at the Headquarters of the UN in Manhattan. Eric and Monica looked at each other in surprise, astonished at this unexpected honour. What would it mean?

There was no way of not accepting the invitation, so just to be sure, Monica decided to postpone sending the wedding invitations till after the meeting. They were invited for the Friday afternoon the following week.

Eric took the opportunity to book a weekend of indulgence at a resort on Long Island, a kind of mini- honeymoon. "This time, accidental meetings with study-mates in the lobby will not be accepted!" Eric warned.

They were obviously expected at the UN Headquarters and were ushered into the waiting room of the Secretary General without delay. Exactly on time, the door to his offices opened and Dr Vigneron met them with outstretched hands.

He took both their hands in his and said: "I have been looking forward to meet you two, please come in and join me for afternoon tea."

A table had been set for three near a window with a great view of Manhattan. All kinds of refreshments and snacks were displayed. They followed Dr Vigneron's example and helped themselves while listening to the secretary- general telling them how impressed the world was with the changes that were happening in US society.

He said that he was not thinking of the economic aspect, although that played an important role. He meant the increasing positive attitudes of many citizens; the statistics that showed less crime and less violence in the streets and more support for charities. The change was slow but the trend was there and people seemed to believe in it.

"I learned from President Charles Brown that you and your team were instrumental in this, and I would like to learn more. Large parts of the world are in worse circumstances than the USA ever was. My hands are tied. The Security Council has not been able to agree on measurements necessary to achieve peace and stability in those parts. If we must call in the help of a computer, then so be it. But how that would be possible, I don't really understand and I wonder if you can help."

For a long while, nothing was said. Eric and Monica looked at each other with doubt in their eyes, and then Eric hesitantly began to formulate a response:

"Thank you, Mr. Secretary General, We are honoured by your request. My first reaction, sir, is that this is too big an assignment for us. It is enormous! We are not schooled in world politics and cannot oversee the consequences of a direction taken based on a computer's results . . ." His voice trailed off.

"I have been considering that too", the Secretary General said. "But you know, people, that are involved with the United Nations on a day to day basis, can get bogged down in their way of thinking. They mostly come from a public service background and many have the regrettable attitude of "play it safe."

"If you were to study the UN charter and look at it with fresh eyes, maybe you can see new ways of possible co-operation between the nations."

"I think . . ." Eric looked questioningly at Monica, "I think we are both intrigued and, if we could get access to all records of the meetings of the United Nations, especially of the Security Council and the General Assembly, then I for one, would like to discuss it with our team. What about you, Monica?"

Monica was happy to agree and said,

"I want to thank you, sir, for your trust in us. The possibility of helping the world to become a better place is intoxicating. I am in! I will definitely have to brush up on my knowledge of international law, but am eager to do so."

The friendly face of the secretary- general showed relief.

"I am truly thankful. The present circumstances all over the world are so critical. Hunger, wars, and environmental disasters, keep displacing people in numbers unprecedented. Our leaders are searching for new ideas, possible solutions. Maybe this is the time that nations are open for a change of procedure so that we can get things done. "This meeting will be kept secret as I don't want you to be under unnecessary pressure, but please think about it carefully, discuss it with your team and come back to me when you have something to tell. Make sure that you only make appointments through my personal secretary so we can keep this under wraps for the time being."

Their planned mini-honeymoon didn't even last one day! They were both too eager to discuss the meeting with the team. The night went by without much sleep and not for the usual honeymoon reasons, but because they were full of anticipation and couldn't stop talking, coming up with and discarding ideas.

Early the next morning, they called home to make sure Professor Bergsteyn and Anthony were not going anywhere. A few hours later, they were home to tell them about the new challenge Dr Vigneron had presented them with.

After the enormity of it had sunk in, Anthony burst out,

"What does the world want? How can we know?"

"It is overwhelming", admitted Monica. "There will be as many wants and needs as there are people. We must find a golden middle -way. Our main aim would have to be to improve the liveability of the world for all of its people." She continued,

"I want to tell you about a presentation I went to recently. It was about the consequences of climate change. During question time, there was one question that seemed to be on most people's mind, 'What can I do?' The answer stuck with me, 'Educate, educate, educate. Teach your children by example not to be egoistic, teach them ethics and moral standards, compassion and about the effect of everything they do or don't do.' I believe that it is not only us, common people, that have to teach our children, but our leaders also have to lead by example and teach their citizens."

"It sounds to me that you guys have already started", said Eric. "But first, we have to discuss if we are really willing to commit ourselves. It will mean that we have to invest lots of time and energy to give it our best shot."

The rest of that Saturday was spent throwing up all possible objections and things that could go wrong. One by one they discussed them, and by Sunday afternoon they decided that they could live with them. They wanted this—, they were committed!

The next morning, Eric put a call through to Dr Vigneron's personal secretary who promised to pass on the request for a return call to the Secretary General. He called back the same day. Eric told the secretary general that he and his team were keen to give it a serious try.

"We are committed, sir, to the challenge. Now we need to talk about the practical things. As you probably know, for the American experiment, we were lucky to obtain a relatively cheap supercomputer that we installed in my factory. The US government was not involved at that stage. They only bought the computer from us after Congress voted for it. For this experiment, I am again prepared to buy a supercomputer first and pay all on-going costs and, like the first one, install it in my factory hall, which has not been used since. The UN can compensate me later. Or, would you prefer that the UN bought the computer and have it installed at the UN Headquarters? Please do realise that the installation is quite a job, and it will be difficult to keep it secret while we are working with it. It needs a good- sized room with either a big reliable air-conditioned cooling system, or a more complicated and power-hungry liquid cooling system. Either of them will cost a big amount of electrical power."

"Thanks for taking it on, Eric, and yes, because we'd like to keep it under wraps for the time being, I appreciate your offer to keep everything at your factory, and of course, you will get compensated, successful or not, that is my problem! Please keep me informed about the cost."

With that part settled, Eric returned to the team to report the agreement. He told them that he would use the profit made on the sale of the supercomputer help pay for another. Danny would be contacted and offered his former job back. Hopefully by now, the technical team he was supervising would be sufficiently experienced to take over. His old team needed him to search and look after the best supercomputer he could find within their means.

Monica said she was willing to invest a big part of her money as well if more was needed. And so, life went back to a similar routine as before:

Professor Bergsteyn minimised his workload as much as possible. He dived into the political philosophy as taught in different parts of the world to find a common ground.

Anthony and Monica tried to come up with the kind of programs that would be needed. Monica also researched international law, especially the records of the International Court of Justice.

Eric still needed to run his factory but managed to delegate more of his workload, enabling him to spend time on the project.

The wedding and the honeymoon were again postponed.

As before, every Saturday they met for lunch and usually continued to exchange and discuss ideas till after Sunday's dinner. They started tackling questions like: how do we find out and compare the spending on defence around the world so we can calculate how much money could be saved and relocated? And to what kind of programs should that money go?

Many other records had to be researched as well before they could decide on the kind of data that would be needed to enable good decision making.

They also talked a lot about the rapidly deteriorating environment because of climate change, and about the reasons that so little progress had been made.

As an example, Eric related the experiences of Jonathan, the factory's technician. He had worked on the big cargo ships and ocean liners and told Eric that when they leave and enter the harbours, they use diesel oil to limit pollution, but as soon as they are in open sea, they will switch to the cheapest oils they can find. Not only that, most do not keep their general waste on board for disposal as landfill. It is all dumped in the ocean. Even though they now try to control it with international regulations, not a lot has changed. Considering the number of ships that travel the oceans, these habits have caused enormous pollution, one of the main reasons—, apart from plastics and global warming—, that our oceans are in big trouble.

If they could only convince the leaders of the world that the computer is impartial, that its conclusions are only based on factual research, maybe they would agree to accept the necessary changes.

Most of their discussions led back to the same conclusion: peace must be the priority, lasting peace in the world. Only then would countries be willing to cut their defence spending and invest in improving the environment and the lives of their citizens.

"The way the Security Council works, their decisions will never achieve the peace we're looking for", Monica sighed. "We will have to find a way of programming the computer to present convincing arguments for changing their system of voting."

"Wow, that is a controversial idea!" exclaimed the professor. "I wonder if we could make that possible. It might indeed be the only way. But how could one get around the "power of veto" of the five permanent members of the Security Council?"

Eric replied that there seemed to be a way around it.

"Monica showed me Resolution 377A[1] of the United Nations General Assembly, the "Uniting for Peace" resolution of 1950, it states that,

". . . if the Security Council, because of lack of unanimity of the permanent members, fails to exercise its primary responsibility for the maintenance of international peace and security in any case where there appears to be a threat to the peace, breach of the peace, or act of aggression, the General Assembly shall consider the matter immediately with a view to making appropriate recommendations to Members for collective measures, including in the case of a breach of the peace or act of aggression, the use of armed force when necessary, to maintain or restore international peace and security[2]."

"How about that?!"

"That was 1950!" Anthony exclaimed. "Why has that not been brought into practice?"

It obviously needed more study and they decided to make the 'Uniting for Peace' resolution the focus of their research and discussions. Monica would concentrate her legal research on cases that concerned these powers of the UN.

Many hours were spent on just getting acquainted with the way the United Nations and its many parts work. How the meetings are organised, how they reach decisions and recommendations, and why they seem to lack power to prevent or stop wars raging throughout the world.

---

[1]   United Nations General Assembly Resolution A/RES/377 (V) 3 November 1950
[2]   www.cfr.org/peacekeeping/un-general-assembly-resolution-377-uniting-peace/
      p23588

Eric appeared at the next meeting with printed copies of Chapter 1 and 2 of the UN Charter called "Purposes and Principles"[3]

Article 1

The Purposes of the United Nations are:

1. To maintain international peace and security, and to that end: to take effective collective measures for the prevention and removal of threats to the peace, and for the suppression of acts of aggression or other breaches of the peace, and to bring about by peaceful means, and in conformity with the principles of justice and international law, adjustment or settlement of international disputes or situations which might lead to a breach of the peace;
2. To develop friendly relations among nations based on respect for the principle of equal rights and self-determination of peoples, and to take other appropriate measures to strengthen universal peace;
3. To achieve international co-operation in solving international problems of an economic, social, cultural, or humanitarian character, and in promoting and encouraging respect for human rights and for fundamental freedoms for all without distinction as to race, sex, language, or religion; and
4. To be a centre for harmonizing the actions of nations in the attainment of these common ends.

Article 2

The Organization and its Members, in pursuit of the Purposes stated in Article 1, shall act in accordance with the following Principles.

1. The Organization is based on the principle of the sovereign equality of all its Members.

---

[3] United Nations, *Charter of the United Nations Chapter 1 Articles 1 and 2*, 1945, 1UNTSXVI, available at www.un.org/en/sections/un-charter/chapter-i. accessed 22/11/2016, reprinted with the permission of the United Nations.

2. All Members, in order to ensure to all of them the rights and benefits resulting from membership, shall fulfil in good faith the obligations assumed by them in accordance with the present Charter.

3. All Members shall settle their international disputes by peaceful means in such a manner that international peace and security, and justice, are not endangered.

4. All Members shall refrain in their international relations from the threat or use of force against the territorial integrity or political independence of any state, or in any other manner inconsistent with the Purposes of the United Nations.

5. All Members shall give the United Nations every assistance in any action it takes in accordance with the present Charter, and shall refrain from giving assistance to any state against which the United Nations is taking preventive or enforcement action.

6. The Organization shall ensure that states which are not Members of the United Nations act in accordance with these Principles so far as may be necessary for the maintenance of international peace and security.

Nothing contained in the present Charter shall authorise the United Nations to intervene in matters which are essentially within the domestic jurisdiction of any state or shall require the Members to submit such matters to settlement under the present Charter; but this principle shall not prejudice the application of enforcement measures under Chapter Vll."

"Hang this above your bed or your desk and learn every word." Eric suggested, handing out the copies. "These are the principles that have to be behind every program that we will feed to the computer." During the next meeting, Monica reported that she had studied the effect of the "Uniting for Peace" resolution and found no or little improvement in promoting effective action by the UN to maintain peace in the world. She thought that one of the biggest problems was that many of the small new countries were persuaded, by monetary or other benefits, to vote with the donating country.

Professor Sebastian warned that their greatest problem would be to find solutions all nations would want to implement. Historically, they had developed and grown so differently. Many had present or past disastrous disputes with other nations and would have difficulty trusting them. Other nations have been carved up and differently put together by colonialist powers, forcing people that have little in common to live and govern together.

The deteriorating environment, water, air, and soil will become causes for conflicts and wars and in some cases, already are.

On the other hand, the last fact might also become a unifying factor when even the most powerful countries realise that only co-operation of all nations will give them the best chance of ecological survival.

After much study and intense discussions during their Saturday meetings, they compiled a list of things that would need to happen to give the world a chance of peace:

a) Every country would have to cut its defence spending by 10% per year, with the result that after 10 years, the only army in the world would be an army of UN blue helmets.

b) Professional soldiers that cannot, and will not, do anything else will be encouraged to join the blue helmets in addition to an agreed number of recruits that must be supplied by each country to this army each year.

c) The countries to which UN soldiers belong must support their own people (soldiers) financially.

d) The blue helmeted army will be the best trained in the world by commanders appointed by the UN. They will be trained, not only in fighting, but also in disaster management and ethics. They would be employed to attend immediately to such disasters as caused by an earthquake, tsunami, major bush fire, cyclone, etc. And hopefully, that will become their main task.

e) The UN would be able, when agreed to by the Security Council or, if necessary, by a 2/3 majority of the General Assembly, to send their troops into any country if that country poses a threat to world peace, to stop a civil war or to prevent that country carrying out genocide in their own country. The UN decision will override any possible sovereign laws of that country.

f) When the blue helmets are employed in this way, they will also stay until the situation has been resolved in co-operation with the leaders of that country.

g) The UN will supervise the weapon industry; weapons may only be produced with their permission and, after 10 years, on their orders only. Individual people will not be allowed to own a gun, unless by special permission.

h) The blue helmets will, in principle, not be stationed on their own continent, and never in their own country, to prevent them being personally involved or affected by the conflict. Exceptions can be made for disaster management and translation requirements.

-.-.-.-

CHAPTER 13

It was very satisfying for the team members to see all their ideas together in front of them. If those ideas would ever be translated into reality, a lot of money would be saved all over the world. That money could then be used to train the UN army, to fund their actions, and to be used anywhere else in the world to improve the lives of people.

"Without the need to put up taxes", Eric said.

Professor Bergsteyn reminded them again that a sustainable future for all could only be achieved by the co-operation of all nations.

"It is easy for us to agree on "common goals", but how we can ever get nations to agree if one of the computer's conclusions would be damaging to some of their people in power, or to profitmaking industries, or would be favouring their enemies, is still beyond me at this stage", sighed Sebastian aloud. "Take the first point, "cutting defence spending". How on earth would you persuade a nation if they felt threatened by their neighbours?"

Monica agreed.

"You are right. In my view, it is one of the reasons the Security Council will never agree to those changes. And it will be just as difficult to get 2/3 of the General Assembly to agree. With the Charter as it is, we stand no chance."

The team members looked at each other despairingly.

"I cannot see it working", sighed Monica "This is above our capabilities. What do you say, Eric?"

Eric shook his head,

"Getting the people in the US to support change is a totally different matter than trying to get all nations to agree. I am not optimistic."

Anthony found it the most difficult to admit defeat and said,

"I would like to give it a bit more time, but if you all agree . . ."

"I suggest" Eric said, "that I call Dr Vigneron and tell him that we are close to giving up. I will explain that, if the voting system of the UN cannot be changed, which means changes to a large part of the Charter, we see no need to invest in a very expensive computer. Let's wait for his reaction."

Eric contacted the personal secretary of Dr Vigneron and was asked to report in person. This time he went on his own, thinking that it would all be cancelled. He was however, surprised by the response.

"I more or less expected this", the secretary- general said. "Your conclusions are right. Several times, members have suggested changes to the voting system. Most countries are very protective of their sovereign rights and the five original countries especially do not want to give up their status. I had hoped that the computer could put up such a convincing argument for change that even those countries would come to see it as the only way.

I suggest you make that your main aim. As I said before, Eric, the world is in crisis and I really have the feeling that most of the delegates will be open to change if you can come up with a good formula."

Dr Vigneron argued for some time more, so convincingly that Eric's mood changed to a more positive one. He found a new confidence in their assignment and he accepted, saying,

"We have talked a lot about positive actions the UN could take if those changes were made, but concluded that it would never be possible. The way you put it inspires me to renew our efforts to formulate a program to achieve that result. I am confident my team will agree."

Back home, the team shared a happy dinner, brimming over with new ideas for programming. After putting in so much time and energy, they didn't want to admit defeat.

Eric decided to take the plunge and buy another computer. He got in touch with Danny Lambert to offer him his old job back and to keep his eye out for another supercomputer.

Danny Lambert did not particularly like living in Washington, and being surrounded by bureaucrats. He missed the uncomplicated country life, and the friends he made in Castleburg. He accepted Eric's offer without another thought and would give a month's notice from that day.

It didn't take long before he called that there was an extraordinary supercomputer for sale in New York City. This one, however, was $50 million and did not come with any pre-loaded programs, but its speed and possibilities were amazing. It was for instance capable of modelling scenarios. If you loaded all relevant information, it could display an animated video of the results and that would appeal to many people. This sounded exciting! But the cost might be a big problem. They decided to get more information before going to Dr Vigneron to discuss the price.

Monica, Eric, and Anthony flew over to New York and Danny joined them from Washington. They had lunch together, happily catching up before discussing the things they would have to look for in this computer.

The computer was not much bigger than the one they used before, but more advanced with the added capability of modelling. This could be a great tool in presenting their arguments. Danny, Monica, and Anthony had lots of questions of course. After inspection, Danny was sure there would be no technical problems involved in installing it in the factory hall. It had an air-conditioned cooling system, just like the first one. When Monica and Anthony expressed their confidence in handling the programming system, Eric suggested for them to go out for a coffee while he tried to organise finance. The price was way above his budget. As the United Nations Building was not far away and he called ahead to request an appointment with Dr Vigneron, he returned within an hour with the go-ahead. Dr Vigneron had access to a special account. It had enough funds to pay for half the quoted price. He would have to report on it by the end of the year, but that was still a long way off, so, for the moment, the secret mission was safe. They returned to the computer company where Eric bargained a 10% discount by agreeing to pay half of the $45 million immediately, and the other half on receipt.

Danny decided to take up his holidays by the end of next week. That made it possible for him to leave Washington earlier and oversee the dismantling and transport to Castleburg. And so, it was agreed.

At the end of that month, the computer was ready to run and accept the great amounts of data that needed to be loaded. Conveniently, this could be done from several keyboards at the same time.

They had been so clever to keep copies of the research results that were on the previous computer and after sorting out the international significant ones, they were quickly updated and added to the programs that Monica and Anthony had developed with lots of data from the UN, the International Court of Justice, and the UN Charter.

Assuming that the UN organisation was willing to consider change, and that they would be able to present their proposal to the United Nations Assembly (if only to show how change could be achieved with the help of a computer), the team came up with many suggestions.

They finally agreed that most importantly, the computer should be able to demonstrate the consequences that would be the result of the Security Council refusing to make meaningful changes and thus stay as impotent as present. The demonstration should be based on worldwide scientific research.

Then they would also have the computer show how positively the world would be affected by the proposed changes, based again on worldwide scientific research.

Antony said,

"We could compare the world to a living body. The scientists teach us that a healthy body has 100 trillion microbes in the gut. Losing continuously more of them because of an unhealthy diet and lifestyle makes the body susceptible to many diseases. Every time the world loses a species, whole series of other creatures follow the same fate. That's why it's high time to change our bad habits and restore and preserve a healthy environment."

-·-·-·-

CHAPTER 14

The team decided to concentrate their efforts on creating a presentation of the consequences that would be the result if the UN should continue as it is. They collected all relevant information, research, statistics, and history of action taken that they could find on the records of governments, charities, universities and other scientific bodies throughout the world.

The computer, named *'Resolve'* by Danny, was then loaded with the sad realities of the world:

a) The cost of wars and conflicts caused by religious differences, racism, environmental factors, and expansion greed to civilians, the country's infrastructure and the environment.

b) The displacement of people, their misery, the dangerous journeys they undertake to escape wars, conflict and/or poverty, the resulting loss of lives, the huge profits made by people smugglers, the financial costs for the taxpayer in the countries that receive them causing an increase in racism and discrimination.

c) The human trafficking for sex, slave labour and child abuse, again causing terrible misery but making huge profits for the traffickers.

d) The globalisation push that disadvantages many people while providing enormous profits to mega corporations and some individuals.

e) The 'war on drugs' that encourages criminality more than rehabilitation.

f) The problems countries have, when they emerge from wars or environmental destruction, in finding help to rebuild their communities with new investments and ecological recovery.

g) The environmental degradation that cannot be reversed as global warming had caused it. For the last decades, many countries had been searching for ways to limit global warming to no more than 2% but failed miserably.

After ordering *Resolve* to process all this information and produce a comprehensive summary of probable consequences in 20 years' time, they watched in horror a graphic display of the devastating development of an environment failing to support the conditions that guarantee the survival of the human race.

It brought tears to Monica's eyes, while Anthony tried hard not to join her.

Eric's temper that had been building up during the display culminated in an angry outburst blaming each and every organisation, including religion, of misleading the people they were supposed to guide and look after, mostly only for power and greed.

Sebastian reminded him then of their assignment and that they had a once-in-a-lifetime-chance to make a difference if they controlled their anger and sought the co-operation of those people and organizations he was blaming.

"Please don't forget that business and religion also have brought a lot of good. The 'Golden Rule' is the same for all or most of the religions."

"Sorry to be so ignorant", Danny said. "But what is the 'Golden Rule?'"

"Don't do to others what you don't want others do to you", Sebastian answered and he added,

"We will still have to appeal to people's self-interest. Making a profit is not inherently bad. You yourself like to make a tidy profit, Eric. A profit shouldn't however be made at a cost to the environment. Corporations, and individuals too, should learn how to spend and invest their capital better to ensure their own future and that of their offspring. We should also remind ourselves that a by-product of an improved economy that benefits all people appears to be that people have less babies, so the world population could become stable."

The short talk of the professor had a healthy effect on the team members and Eric said,

"OK, you are right professor, sorry. I was very affected by what was shown. I also thought back again to the story of the *'Tragedy of the Commons'*. What hope do we have, given human nature as it is? At present, I am at a loss and don't know how to get back to a more positive state of mind, Sebastian."

Professor Sebastian replied,

"Thanks for reminding me of that story. I wonder if Anthony could program the story of the *'Tragedy of the Commons'* in and show an animated version? It could help to change the rigid thinking of the market fundamentalists. Like all fundamentalists, they will be the hardest to convince.

"We should ask ourselves, as inhabitants of the so-called developed countries, why are we so short-sighted and egoistic that we continue to add to our already over-abundant possessions while our children and grandchildren are certain to suffer from the results of the overuse of earth's resources?"

Without waiting for a reply, Sebastian continued, holding their attention,

"Yes! My question reminds me of an article I discovered, written by Herschel Elliott. It is about the "**Tragedy of the Commons**". Now, where is it?" he said impatiently rummaging through his papers. "Got it!" he exclaimed triumphantly, holding some papers up in the air.

"Please listen. It is called "**A General Statement of the Tragedy of the Commons**"[4], and Sebastian started to read,

"Almost everyone recognizes that we must preserve our national heritage -- our parks and wildlife, our farms, our wetlands and forests.

And few dare to doubt that equal justice and universal human rights are essential axioms of morality. Simultaneously, people accept the necessity of protecting the environment and they also assume the moral obligation that every human being has an equal right to health, education, and employment, regardless of where a person is born or from where that person is fleeing hardship or persecution. To satisfy these demands, it becomes a moral necessity to create more jobs, to build more housing, to expand the infrastructure, to produce more food

---

[4]   Elliott. Herschel "A General Statement of the Tragedy of the Commons" (1997) dieoff.org/page121.htm, parts have been reprinted with the permission of the author.

and water, and to provide more sanitation, health care, and educational facilities.

The ethical implications of the Earth's finitude are made clear in one of the world's great essays. The author conducts a simple-seeming thought experiment in which he proves that any ethics is mistaken if it allows a growing population steadily to increase its exploitation of the ecosystem which supports it . . . because it leads to the destruction of the biological resources on which survival depends; it lets people act in ways that make all further ethical behaviour impossible. The essay in which this fundamental flaw in modern Western moral thinking is demonstrated in Garrett Hardin's *"The Tragedy of the Commons"*[5].

Specifically, the '*Tragedy of the Commons*' demonstrates that all behaviour is conditional on the size of the human population and the availability of material resources."

Sebastian looked up from his papers and, after a sip of water, said

said "Just to be clear, Herschel Elliot's essay refers to a 2nd 'Tragedy of the Commons' written by Garrett Hardin who was inspired by the original parable, we talked about earlier. I encourage you to read the whole article, but for the moment I think it is sufficient to end with parts of Herschel Elliott's own summary[6].

I find it inspiring and think you will too." And he continued his reading,

""Now for the first time in history, the cumulative effect of human activity has become a major and perhaps the dominant force affecting the Earth's ecosystems . . . a drastic change is necessary in the way in which ethics itself is conceived and moral practices are justified.

Ethical behaviour must be relative to its most important goal— -- to protect and sustain the Earth's diverse, yet mutually supporting system of living things. Thereafter, the secondary goal of ethics may be addressed, namely, to maximize the quality of human life.

Ecosystems are in dynamic equilibrium. In addition, technology and human institutions are constantly evolving in novel and unpredictable

---

[5]   Hardin. Garrett "The Tragedy of the Commons" Science. Vol.162. December 1968 pp. 1243-1248

[6]   Elliott. Herschel "A General Statement of the Tragedy of the Commons. A summary and Overview" (1997) dieoff.org/page121.htm, parts have been reprinted with the permission of the author

ways. Furthermore, living things must compete with each other for space and resources; yet, each organism also depends symbiotically on the well-being of the whole for its own survival and well-being. Indeed, the welfare of all organisms— – including human beings— – is causally dependent on the health and stability of the ecosystems which sustain them. As a consequence, the stability and well-being of the Earth's bio-system has moral priority over the welfare of any of its parts including the needs and interests of human societies and individuals. Although biological human behaviour has a veto over what people may want and hope, empirical knowledge can guide human behaviour. And that knowledge clearly indicates that holistic planning and societally enforced constraints are the means to prevent the tragic breakdown of the Earth's bio-system. When thus grounded in the nature and needs of life ethics can take its place among all the other human endeavours: science, medicine, technology, art, music and literature.'""

Sebastian looked around at the thoughtful faces.

"We cannot have better arguments for the need of 'enforced constraint'."

Eric thanked Sebastian for this very enlightening article, agreeing that it would be very helpful in formulating their argument. However, he still doubted if they could convince any nation to accept voluntarily constraints on their growth.

"That's why we need to find a way to empower the UN", Monica argued. "It's true that no country is going to accept limitations to protect other parts of the globe, unless we appeal to their self-interest. We need to convince them that our planet, and thus their own country, has a chance of survival if countries will accept rules and regulations, agreed on by a 2/3 majority in the General Assembly of the UN and to be enforced by the UN peace keepers" army."

"If we would only be able to achieve that", Eric sighed. "How can we present a convincing case?"

"I have been studying the cases that concern the powers of the UN to employ the blue helmets to enforce the peace", Monica said. "They do have these powers but they're hardly used and never in countries in which one or more of the five original countries are involved in one way or another. Firstly, we must convince all UN members of three things,

1./ They are looking the facts in the face

2./ We are at the point of no return and
3./ Priority must be given to "world peace"."

"If we're able to do that, they could be open for change to the voting system and enable the UN to take quick and decisive action when necessary."

"That's it! That is how we should go about it", Eric said. "We have seen and were all upset when we saw the negative results of no action at all. We now need to demonstrate how the world can be saved if the necessary majority of nations votes to empower the UN."

"That will be easier said than done", Monica and Anthony said at the same time.

"Come on, you know-all computer nerds!" the professor said. "We have done it before. We used positive outcomes in our first trial to help the American Government see the benefits. We can do that again. Just as there is much information about future scenarios if we keep polluting as we are doing now, there are also many studies about the positive impacts on global warming if all nations could agree to cut down on pollution, stop using coal for energy, stop cutting down forests, using damaging chemicals and so forth. You can hopefully show a positive effect on the environment, especially if, at the same time, the global community would invest massively in rehabilitation, alternative energy, and international distribution. There has been research and tests to find out how long it will take for nature to recover, and pollution to decrease after an environmental disaster and/or war."

"Of course," Eric said with relief. "That was our plan from the beginning, we got too negative after the first scenario and forgot about it. If we can show in animation how both outcomes are likely to affect us all, it will clearly demonstrate how impotent the world, represented in the United Nations, has been to agree on anything else than marginal measurements. Then we might convince them of the importance to facilitate a change to the voting system."

"I have been thinking", Anthony said, "about how a change to the voting system could be achieved. It would have to be by a change to Chapter 14 of the Charter, the chapter that regulates voting. What if we propose that countries with more than 10 million people have one vote?

Countries with a smaller population must get together so that they also represent at least 10 million people to have one shared vote.

By my estimation, that should change the total number of votes from nearly 200 to approximately 120. It seems to me a fairer distribution of the votes that represent the world's population. It would make the communication simpler and a 2/3 majority much more likely. The rule that the five original countries have to agree with all security decisions should be abolished at the same time!"

They agreed that these changes would set the stage for the UN to get on with the things that should be done to save the planet's environment for the survival of the species.

"A superbly trained and equipped blue helmet force that can be employed immediately in an area after a disaster, or in a conflict area before the conflict escalates, who could argue against that?", wondered Eric.

They continued to talk about how it might become possible for all nations to agree to delegate some of their powers to the United Nations. One military force supplied with soldiers from each voting country or combination of countries, led by experienced generals appointed by the Security Council. This force should be trained thoroughly in international matters so they would not only learn to respect the heritage of all army personnel they work with but also be sensitive to the culture of the people in the area they are deployed in. They"ll be accountable to the UN, and criminal matters will be dealt with through a special department of the International Court of Justice.

They estimated that it should be possible to achieve all of this within 10 years with all countries progressively decreasing their defence spending and investing the savings. Progressively, the UN would take over the control over weapon production. At the end of this ten-year period, weapons would only be able to be produced on order of, or with the permission from the United Nations. Those that had to stop producing weapons would be assisted and supervised by the UN in changing to an environmentally friendly industry. Individuals would not be allowed to own weapons unless needed in their profession. They would be "background checked" and monitored.

It took them a long time to translate most of their ideas into computer language, they even flirted with the Ten Commandments, the Magna Carta and the "good government" as Socrates described it.

When they performed their next test session, the outcome was much more positive when the agreed conditions were met. Be it that some of the outcomes astonished them. For instance, finding solutions for all the displaced people was not the priority anymore, but top of the list was the enforcing of peace by ordering the blue helmets to massively invade warring countries, enforce peace, supervise negotiations between warring parties and re-establish basic living standards. The result would be that most displaced people would want to return to their home countries and assist in the rehabilitation. Obviously, the blue helmets would have to stay in those countries until they were satisfied that there would be a lasting peace. This would be the first step on the way to improve the survival chances of all living beings. Much more time and money would become available to tackle climate change and invest in making the world sustainable

It still took months and months to fine-tune the computer programs. In the meantime, the world was not at a standstill. The programs had to be continuously updated with new research data. They noticed with alarm that the number of natural disasters was increasing rapidly. The West Coast of Europe experienced a devastating tsunami. Cities were wiped off the map and thousands of people lost their lives.

As usual, climate change badly affected island nations and other small countries, but it became clear that large countries and continents were now also struggling to recover from disasters like earthquakes, hurricanes, fires and floods, the strength of which they had not experienced before.

-.-.-.-

CHAPTER 15

When the Secretary General flew in by helicopter, there was more tension in the air than when they made their presentation to the President of the USA. The responsibility for a good outcome weighed heavily on their minds and although they had high expectations of how their experiment would be received when they called for the meeting, they were now full of doubt. They knew that Dr Vigneron was a highly intelligent man. He could ask questions they might not be prepared for.

Eric explained their plan to the Secretary General. After a demonstration and brief explanation of the programs on the computer, Dr Vigneron could ask *Resolve*—, as was now the computer's official name—, some actual questions that would fall within the framework of those programs. The whole process, including answers and visual displays from *Resolve* would be filmed and documented by Monica and Anthony. If Dr Vigneron was satisfied with the resulting documentary, they suggested, he could show it to the Security Council, the General Assembly or to all members combined, whatever he thought would be most effective.

The first question Dr Vigneron asked the computer was, "What to do about the enormous refugee problems in the world?"

The answer astonished the hardened diplomat.

"I did not expect this solution", he said. "But of course, it is right. The problems are all connected and interwoven. Most people would prefer to stay in or return to their own place if it could be made safe and liveable. With the help of *Resolve*, we might find a way to empower the UN."

More questions followed, and *Resolve* performed well. Dr Vigneron was very impressed.

"Congratulations, team! You did a great job and I am sold."

If he could convince the necessary majority of the UN members that change was essential for the survival of each one of their countries, that there was no other solution, the UN would buy the computer and take over further programming.

After viewing and accepting the documentary of his visit, Secretary General Vigneron gave a passionate speech before a joint sitting of the United Nations General Assembly and Security Council. Then he introduced the screening of the documentary. The audience was spell-bound and very quiet after watching the animated display of the non-action and action scenarios.

A large majority voted for change, which meant that Dr Vigneron would have no trouble finding the money for the computer.

Only two of the permanent members of the Security Council had refrained from voting. This was a better result than expected, as those powerful countries were very much involved in several wars that were going on. Dr Vigneron managed to persuade them to have another look at the whole set up and systems, and convince them of the impartiality of the process. They confessed that they themselves and many people in their government were very worried about the future. However, they foresaw big problems in convincing their top leaders and security agency. Dr Vigneron promised to fly out with them and show their governments not only the benefits of world co-operation but also the fact that there simply was no other way. The status quo is the road to destruction of the conditions necessary to support human life in every part of the world! Even if their part would last the longest, what would be the point?

Dr Vigneron did not limit his appeal to the UN, but released the videos of both scenarios to all TV stations in the world and to the activist organisations that used the internet to organise protest marches and mobilise people into sending messages to governments etc. Many of those pressure groups worked together and their memberships grew rapidly. Also, many business organisations and unions reacted positively.

The result was a massive movement all over the world, even in countries where demonstrations were not allowed and penalties were harsh. Their motto was that, if we all demonstrate, there is not much they can do and without change, we are all doomed eventually.

There were people in many governments that had wanted change for a long time. They now felt empowered by the will of the people and so from inside and outside, most governments were pressured to support the UN fully, financially, as well as with their own policies and legislation.

Although sad to leave the Castleburg community again, Danny was willing to accompany the computer *Resolve* to New York. The supercomputer was his passion and at least in the mega city New York, he wouldn't be bumping into bureaucrats all the time. He kept the house he recently bought as he was planning to spend most of his holidays back in his favourite country town.

To the team members, the success was a big relief and gave them a wonderful feeling of achievement. They had been an essential part of the start of real co-operation throughout the world, giving hope to humanity.

Like after the first time they had successfully completed their assignment, they needed time together to unwind and come back to reality. They also had to cope with their new status as celebrities and were interviewed many times. To their relief, the events of the world, the changes that were implemented, the successes and the mishaps, soon took over the attention of the news hounds.

Eventually all four went happily back to their daily tasks. Eric and Monica had a beautiful wedding and a lovely honeymoon at last.

Within the 10 years of transition to overall peace, as the team had proposed and was accepted by the UN, the world had changed its course, and faster than expected, it became a better place with a liveable future.

THE END

www.ingramcontent.com/pod-product-compliance
Lightning Source LLC
Chambersburg PA
CBHW021146070326
40689CB00044B/1202